Media and Their Publics

Michael Higgins

Mc Graw Hill   Open University Press

Open University Press
McGraw-Hill Education
McGraw-Hill House
Shoppenhangers Road
Maidenhead
Berkshire
England
SL6 2QL

email: enquiries@openup.co.uk
world wide web: www.openup.co.uk

and Two Penn Plaza, New York, NY 10121-2289, USA

First published 2008

A catalogue record of this book is available from the British Library

ISBN-10: 0335219292 (pb)   0335219306 (hb)
ISBN-13: 9780335219292 (pb)   9780335219308 (hb)

Library of Congress Cataloguing-in-Publication Data
CIP data applied for

Fictitious names of companies, products, people, characters and/or data that may be used herein (in case studies or in examples) are not intended to represent any real individual, company, product or event.

Typeset by BookEns Ltd, Royston, Herts.
Printed in the UK by Bell and Bain Ltd, Glasgow

The **McGraw·Hill** Companies

Contents

Acknowledgements

I am grateful to the staff at Open University Press, past and present, for their patience and advice in the composition of this book. Thanks in particular to Chris Cudmore, who encouraged the original idea and guided much of the preparation, as well as to Louise Caswell, Jack Fray and Melanie Havelock.

What clarity there is in this book owes a great deal to my numerous conversations and arguments with Angela Smith of the University of Sunderland, who was also a critical reader and reservoir of references, data and coffee breaks. Karin Wahl-Jorgensen of Cardiff University also provided insightful comments on a number of the chapters.

I owe a considerable debt to the Centre for Research in Media and Cultural Studies at the University of Sunderland, where much of this work was undertaken and who were supportive in providing a semester's study leave. Thank you in particular to the Centre management of John Storey and Shaun Moores, as well as Andrew Crisell, Angela Werndly, Niall Richardson, Clarissa Smith, Amir Saeed, Rob Jewitt, John-Paul Green and Monika Metyková. Thank you also to my new colleagues at the University of Strathclyde: in particular, Nigel Fabb, David Goldie, Faye Hammill, Tereza McLaughlin-Vanova, Brian McNair, Martin Montgomery and Eamonn O'Neill.

Others that have been helpful at various stages include Valentina Cardo, Colin Cremin, Stephen Cushion, Nick Couldry, Philip Drake, Yusaf Ibrahim, Bethany Klein, Derek Mckiernan, Kerry Moore, Michael Pickering, Andy Ruddock, Gary and Julie Russell, Heather Savigny, Niamh Stack, James Stanyer, John Street, Mick Temple, Claire Wardle, Mark Wheeler and Dominic Wring.

I'm afraid any blame for the content lies with me.

As always, the greatest thanks are due to my parents, Margaret and Thomas Higgins.

1 Issues of the public

Introduction

An operational idea of what constitutes 'the public' is a central component of the operation of media, and yet it comes laden with assumptions. This chapter will begin a book dedicated to this vital concept by sketching out the key issues involving media and the various constructions of public. We will unpick our contemporary understanding of the public by examining its development through the classical and modern periods, assessing the importance of maintaining a politically engaged view of the public and public conduct – as they relate to media in particular. Much of what is to come will assume that the public operates as an element of what Norman Fairclough (1995) and others have described as 'media discourse' in that it presents a form of representation that contributes to the exercise and regulation of power. In introducing the issues to come, this chapter will also emphasize and begin to explore the notion of 'governance' as a potential resource in examining the use of the public in media, especially with regard to the extent to which ideas of the public have become bound up with normative judgements of media performance and ethics. To this end, the case of 'public service' media will be examined in detail. We will then take the opportunity to summarize how the rest of the book will develop these themes and present a critical appraisal of how the nebulous concept of public is key to comprehending what media do – and what they ought to do.

When Tony Bennett et al. (2005) revisited Raymond Williams's idea of compiling a critical 'keywords' of contemporary social and cultural usage, they included the term 'public' and appointed renowned scholar Craig Calhoun to the task. Perhaps, the surprise might have been that the word was not included in Williams's (1983) original selection. From 'public nuisance' to 'public art' to 'public prosecutor', the lexicon of publicness arises in a variety of cultural, political, legal and bureaucratic contexts, normally with associations of the civil realm. Yet despite the ease with which the term moves from one context to the next, 'public' stands out as an *overtly* significant word, and never more than when it is used in relation to media and communication industries. There is public access television and public service broadcasting, as well as public participation media and media operating in the public interest. If there is one factor that unites many of these, it is that the public is often invoked in contexts of judgement or of holding to aesthetic, moral or political account. This is as true whether the judgement is said to be on the part of 'the public' itself, as with opinion polls of various sorts (Lewis 2001), or whether it is on the part of professionals and regulators claiming to maintain 'public interest' (Blumler and Hoffman-Riem 1992: 220–1; McQuail 1994: 241; Harcup 2007). Indeed, John Rawls (1996: 68) comments that the concept is so central to legitimizing political power that even political demagogues fashion their rhetoric around 'the power of the public'. To a larger extent, the 'public' is there to be brandished as a warrant of interrogation, and demonstrable engagement with the public becomes an indicator of adequate media performance.

This sense of the public is bound up in an attitude to social commitment that is as long established as civil society, but it is important not to assume this has always been equated with political empowerment. In Homer's Ancient Greek epic poem Odyssey, in seeking to convince the reader of the vileness of the Cyclops – a creature the narrative has yet to reveal – Homer cites the monster's civic irresponsibility. The Cyclops and its kin are described as a collection of 'arrogant, lawless beings' with 'no assemblies to debate in', living in circumstances in which 'the head of each family heeds no other, but makes his own ordinances for wife and children' (Homer 1980: 101). That they also like to dine on human beings warrants a mention later, but only after the listener is invited to contemplate with horror that the Cyclops have no public life – this being the very essence of civilization. Yet, John Durham Peters (1995: 7) points out, discourses of public to predominate in the Greece or Rome of antiquity were bound up with the mere 'exhibition' of virtue; a willingness to be exposed to the judgement of 'the people'. In this sense, Peters argues, conceptions of the classical public as onlookers for the display of 'shame and glory', rather than as a dynamic force, resemble the view of the public taken by the feudal rulers of the high middle ages, concerned in embodied display of power rather than appearing to represent the populace. As Carroll Glynn et al. (2004: 42) remark, it is against this background that Machiavelli's *The Prince* presented as such an effective instruction manual for public conduct. Throughout, public display has been bound up with acceptable modes of conduct, but Peters (1995: 8) insists that it was not until the eighteenth century that ideas of the public began to coalesce around contemporary ideas of citizenship and political inclusion: a development we will discuss in Chapter 2's section on the public sphere.

Discussion of the public since the eighteenth century may well have taken place within an inclusive political idiom, but its use has extended in ways that come neither from traditional politics nor are especially inclusive. Calhoun (2005: 283) shows how other circumstances began to develop that saw public used in a bureaucratic sense to mean the sum of those outside of an immediate professional or administrative circle, but who nevertheless live under its jurisdiction. It is easy to see the public used in this way on signs specifying the terms of admission for 'members of the public', or where a regulatory body or police force claims to be driven by the 'protection of the public'. But this unity and belonging has always come with conditions. As Calhoun points out, admittance to the status of a 'public person' during the eighteenth century demanded adequate demonstration of material success and intellect, and it is arguably still the case that entrance to a public building, and even representation from a regulatory body, requires a veneer of convention-ality that may be termed 'public respectability'. This means that, to different and fluctuating extents, those social groups that Antonio Gramsci (1971: 52) refers to as 'subaltern' and without prospect of coming to dominance, such as the working classes, women, racial and ethnic minority groups are often seen to be excluded from what may be described as a dominant public.

What unites these formations of public is that they are necessarily schemes of representing the population at large by focusing on particular groups or individuals in ways that are bound up with cultural and political power. So being an active and influential member of a public implies a set of civic and cultural practices that are normally the preserve of a relative minority. Just as civic buildings are designed to allow some degree of public access, their architecture is designed to smother this engagement in the grandeur of authority. Even when the procedures are not purposeful, access to legitimated forms of public conduct is strategically distributed among perceived intellectual elites and opinion leaders. This articulation between public and the exercise of power should be seen alongside the prominence of the public in everyday media language and in media policy. In terms of social and cultural politics, mention of the public seems to confirm Regis Debray's (1983: 140) argument that political interests and ideologies operate within and depend upon references to the human collective.

All in all, while the term, 'the public', resonates as an element of everyday discourse, its use hides any number of contradictions. For one thing, there is the distinction that Jürgen Habermas (2004) makes between what are two quite different forms of public engagement. There is on the one hand the option of seeking to become a public personality, in a manner commonly associated mainly with the 'celebrities' of the cultural realm, but also as an ambition of politicians and those seeking administrative power (Street 2004). Here, a 'self conscious and strategic' breach is made between the public and private to display a crafted 'persona' as an item of public interest (Corner 2003). Another strategy described by Habermas (2004), and one more in keeping with his own thinking on political rationality, is the option of engaging in the deliberative processes associated with his conception of what we will go on to call 'the public sphere'. Here, an individual will listen to and offer suggestions on matters of common interest, so that ideas should stand or fall based on their own strengths or weaknesses. In such a case, public engagement is a matter of contributing to a shared pool of intelligence, leaving issues of personality – celebrated or otherwise – as irrelevant and potentially counterproductive. But our concern here is more with the dynamics of the relationship between publicness and media than with those specific debates on forms of argument, sincerity and authenticity. And this relationship is an important one, as John Corner et al. (1997: 6) remind us when they point out that talk of 'the public' often works to blur the boundaries between the interests of the citizenry and the interests of those in power.

Public as discourse

Already, we have established that the use of 'public' – in media and elsewhere – is widespread, and also that the ideas behind the use of public are complex and significant. It is important, then, to think about the way public is used as a means of representing social meaning. Over the last few decades, the term 'discourse' has emerged as a means of describing the place of representation in establishing and reproducing social relations. In book length interrogations of the term, both Diane Macdonell (1986) and Sara Mills (1997) acknowledge the divergent and contradictory developments in the use of the term 'discourse'. There are those interested in the organization of language as a sensemaking activity that use discourse in a broad sense to refer to the capacity of language to make meaning 'above the sentence' (see Stubbs 1983), and then there are critical theorists such as Michel Foucault (1970, 1972) as well as Barry Hindess and Paul Hirst (1977) who use discourse to describe the various institutional and relational strategies of exercising power. Elements of both approaches unite in the 'critical discourse analysis' approach, which attempts a systematic scrutiny of the composition and grammar of socially and politically significant texts (Fairclough 1995; Fairclough and Wodak 1997). As discourse, the public therefore links representation and power. As the rest of the book comes to look at the discursiveness of the public in media, we can consider its persuasive power – looking at the way that individuals and groups present a convincing or authentic face in the media – and will be in a position to discuss formal, political or social power, where arrangements of signification around the public allow institutions and individuals to exercise forms of dominance.

Through the work of Foucault in particular, it has become apparent that the 'discursive regimes' that underlie dominant orders of signification and access to truth and legitimacy develop with a particular purpose: namely, to accommodate the needs of institutions of social control and organization, such as hospitals and prisons (Foucault 1973, 1977). Similarly, argues Gareth Palmer (2003), media texts are complicit in discursive practices that reflect the political interests and production imperatives of the media institutions themselves. According to John Thompson, however, as much as any commitment to discursive control this is driven by the technical capacities of media. As Thompson points out, the boundaries of public discussion have been driven by the growth of media, but in a way that yokes the constitution of public life with access to technology. Arguing that public life has undergone a 'transformation of visibility', Thompson (1995: 125-6) claims that media technology releases public engagement from the constraints of 'co-presence'. He writes that 'the publicness of individuals, actions or events is no longer linked to the sharing of a common locale'. However, an emphasis on mediation of the public sphere has turned what may have been an extension of public conduct into a set of defining imperatives of publicness. Public conduct has itself become the capacity to address absent others and place contributions on record, meaning that the integration of media has shifted the criteria needed to constitute a public act (Thompson 1995: 127). The advent of mass media, in other words, has served to alter the very terms by which we can understand public conduct, in a way that leaves the public sphere exposed to what Habermas (1989: 163) describes as a 'private form of appropriation' (see also Thompson 1995: 131-2).

Even though Richard Sennett (2002: 89) describes it as a comparatively novel invention, with an even more recent vintage than our idea of the public, it is necessary to say something about what Habermas refers to as the private. According to Thompson (1995: 123), 'a public act is a visible act, performed openly so that everyone can see; a private act is invisible, an act performed secretly and behind closed doors'. The capacity to be a member of a public assumes latitude to maintain some measure of privacy, a place where one may be relatively insulated from state surveillance and interference (Hannay 2005: 7). Albeit quite wrongly in his view, Sennett (2002: 4) describes how the private is venerated as an oasis of reflection, transcendence and authenticity: the truth behind the artifice of publicness. Warren and Brandeis' (1890)

Harvard Law Review essay 'The right to privacy', speaking against the capacity of high speed photography to capture the human likeness without consent, offers an early expression of this sanctity for the private as it relates to the publicizing drive of media (in Peters 1999: 174). Much is at stake in our assessment of the private, since it has a dynamic relationship with the performance of the public. It will become apparent that the realm of the public is often used to resolve problems and disputes associated with the private, and the private is routinely presented as the source of sincerity. The chapters to come will see this relationship between the public and private manifest in performances of public conduct: in the constructed relationships between audiences and media professionals, and in the positioning of hosts, news presenters and hired experts.

The public and governance

As we turn now to the issue of the public and political empowerment, it will be useful for us to reflect upon a number of the interpretations that have developed around the idea of 'governance'. This term has taken on a number of related meanings, and in the area of political science, governance has been used to refer to 'self-governing networks' engaged in the production of agreed political ends (Rhodes 1997; Temple 2000: 321). The debates over governance that concern us most directly arose out of a series of lectures given by Michel Foucault during the late 1970s, in which he explicitly sought to tackle 'the issue of population' and its regulation (Foucault 1991: 87). Foucault (1991: 103) notes that the apparatus of central control is still commonly described in terms of the rule of force, of persuasion, and in ways that draw upon charisma and sovereignty, all of which retain a role in the contemporary political terrain. However, he insists that the pre-eminent means of defining and regulating population are the institutions and practices of government. The definition of 'government' that we are obliged to work with here is a wide one, and is intended to extend beyond the institutions of state policy management to cover the regulation of conduct in general. Colin Gordon (1991: 2) summarizes this Foucauldian view of government as 'a form of activity aiming to shape, guide or affect the conduct of some person or persons'. In part, this was an expansion on Foucault's earlier work on the maintenance of regimes of conduct in prisons, where he fashioned a mode of critique on the imposition of habits of self-policing (Foucault 1977; Ransom 1997: 59). However, as Foucault's attention turned to population, he was obliged to consider the wider issue of how the state as a whole engenders a culture of 'governmentality': that is, how techniques of 'regulation' and 'guidance' (Foucault 2000: 68) we can see in the institution succeed in a more outwardly liberated social context (Gordon 1991: 4).

Also in common with his earlier works, Foucault (1991: 99) argued that the very notion of population is historically contingent. It was, he suggested, the rise of statistics that offered the means to comprehend population as an object of regulation, with the requirements of the economy being the motivating factor. What unfolded was a shift in focus from the apparatuses of the state to the more complex matter of its occupants, and the expressed purpose was to establish how patterns of health and economic conduct at the individual level have demonstrable consequences for the well-being of the state. Repressive tactics of economic control such as taxation and artificial scarcity thus became an integral part of state control, with the ultimate aim of enhancing the interests of controlling authorities by cultivating the healthy and industrious population (Foucault 2000: 69). Success in exercising state power has, in short, become a matter of governance. An important quality of governmentality is that it is less about the imposition of power than the widespread internalization of practices of governing the self and others at the local level. Thus, in spite of the seemingly macro emphasis of population and government, the practices of governance are found in such micro contexts as that of the workplace, the bar-room and the household.

As the book proceeds, we will revisit Foucault's arguments that discourses based upon different forms of public accountability offer deeply embedded means of governing conduct. In his work during the mid-1970s, Foucault (1973, 1977) tried to show how either the gaze of authority, or the ever present belief that one may be under surveillance instils certain forms of subjectivity that places the individual as an object of centralizing and institutionalized systems of power and containment. Foucault's (1984) later work on the history of sexuality went on to look at the role of confession in encouraging the individual to discuss and reflect upon their own selves, so setting themselves within frameworks of morality. The book will show that this has become apparent in mediated forms of public confession – looking at the raft of confession-based talk shows – and will try and explore the implications of the forms of public conduct represented by the participants, the audience and the host.

Public service / public interest

One of the most prominent ways in which media expresses a relation-ship with the public is the manner in which they are held to or maintain a responsibility to the public interest. In the United States, there is a sector made up of media organizations that maintain guiding principles of 'public service', and attracts a limited but symbolically important amount of state funding for doing so. In terms of audience share, public service media in the US does not present as significant a force as it does in countries such as the United Kingdom. Nonetheless, the attachment to public service and the principles of objectivity and balance this entails accords the US public service media an element of prestige, helped by the critical success of PBS programmes such as *The News Hour with Jim Lehrer* and the children's programme *Sesame Street*. The arrangements for public service media, and in particular the provision of partial state funding, were put in place by the passage through Congress of the Public Broadcasting Act of 1967. This Act declares that public interest requires television and radio to be developed for 'instructional, educational, and cultural purposes' and notes ensuring that public interest is adequately served by broadcasters should be a concern of federal government (in Corporation for Public Broadcasting undated). The Corporation for Public Broadcasting was established to distribute government funds to public service stations, to warrant these stations' financial accountability and their diligence towards their area communities, and to ensure content meets the exacting standards the public is entitled to expect (Corporation for Public Broadcasting 2004).

In spite of the determined rhetoric of the 1967 Act, it is important to note that the relationship between government and public service media in the US has not been a steady one, and this has been reflected in the levels of state funding made available. Through the 1970s and into the 1980s, the majority of public service funding came from government. However, the presidency of Ronald Reagan saw the development of a neo-liberal approach to the national economy – one that emphasizes the role of the free market as against the regulatory power of the state – with an attendant suspicion of what came to be seen as the instinct of 'big government' to raise and spend taxes. The negative consequences of the economic neo-liberalism of the 1980s on journalistic and cultural life has been adequately documented elsewhere (see McChesney 1999), and will not need to be rehearsed in full here. Suffice to say, the 'government activism' of the bloated state came to be seen as an inherently bad thing that had to be curbed or made smaller (see Scheuer 2001: 164), and government funding of cultural activities was seen as a good place to begin these processes of reduction. Initial attempts to remove government funding altogether, culminating in the near bankruptcy of public service media in 1983, eventually settled into an arrangement in which much reduced government funding would be supplemented by money from the viewers and listeners, sponsors and other organizations.

Since the shifts in economic policy that characterized the Reagan era were reflected in other national contexts such as the United Kingdom and Australia (see McGuigan 1996; Hutchinson 1999: 157), it is worth dwelling on the arrangements for public service media in the United States and its response to this effort at delegitimation. The US has three main public service radio broadcasters: National Public Radio (NPR), American Public Media and Public Radio International, the largest of which is NPR. NPR is an organization of public radio stations which was founded in 1970 within the terms set out by the Public Broadcasting Act of three years earlier. In 1977, NPR expanded its remit to include managing, training, promoting and representing member stations. The organization operates on a democratic basis, whereby each of the stations (irrespective of size) is allocated one vote at annual board meetings. Representatives are also elected to a board of directors concerned with the day-to-day management of the organization, and a third of this board is made up of lay members of the public. The original aims of NPR placed an emphasis on the provision of programmes for minority groups, with a prominence given to educational material. However, as well as minority cultural programming (including drama and classical music), NPR provides a daily news schedule and current affairs programming including well-known hosts such as Tim Ashbrook of WBUR and Diane Rehm of WAMU. In keeping with the downward trend of public service funding arrangements in general, government funding now accounts for around 2 percent of NPR funding.

In the case of television, the main provider of content is the Public Broadcasting Service (PBS). The PBS was founded in 1969 as a direct consequence of the Public Broadcasting Act, and began operations in late 1970. In common with NPR, the PBS is not a producer of programming, but is rather an amalgamation of member stations operating at the local or state level. Many of these member stations are themselves substantial enterprises, such as the major news stations WETA-TV in Washington, DC, and WPBT in Fort Lauderdale. One of the routine ways in which the PBS exerts its influence is by regulating the peak-time schedules of stations and by retaining copyrights and merchandising options. Although member stations remain free to take content from outside the PBS arrangement, and ordinarily do, the service therefore provides a means by which relatively modest, local stations can integrate public service by situating local content alongside high production news and educational programming, as well as having access to productions by the BBC and other overseas producers.

There is one key point that marks out the public service ethos represented by this form of broadcasting, and this is the distinction that is made between the responsibilities of providing a public service and those conventional considerations of audience measurement which draw mainly upon advertisers' concerns with the numbers and demographic qualities of listeners or viewers. At least by intention, public service media is concerned more with establishing and meeting the needs of the public good than with gathering audiences for the purposes of advertising. In this sense, public service media in the US is intended to address the deficit highlighted by Ben Bagdikian (1985: 98) between a substantial quantity of commercial media outlets and limited 'diversity and richness of content'. In practice, providing this diversity means seeking out those forms of service not provided for under the dominant commercial arrangements. What emerges is therefore a form of public service that sees the public as a series of minority interest groups that have broadcasting needs as yet unfulfilled, especially those needs that are not outwardly shared by commercial or even state interests. National Public Radio, for example, promise in their mission statement that they will 'develop and distribute programs for specific groups', including those seeking adult education, even where such material 'may not have general national relevance'.

As may be said of the public in general, Michael McCauley (2002) writes that the notion of public service has been an ongoing matter of debate. The internalized rhetoric of public service media stresses the importance of the variety and educative value of content. However, the terms and political consequences of this ethos are subject to constant attack from critics across the political and cultural spectrum. One of the arguments against public service media has been that it adopts an overly paternalistic tone in deciding which material is of appropriate value to be of service to the audience. Within a regime of categorization that some see as arbitrary at best, the processes of judgement necessarily limit the types of programming that characterizes public service media. Whatever the decreasing sums involved, this means that some forms of programme are subsidized by government taxes while others – perhaps more popular in terms of viewing figures – have to depend entirely on subscription and advertising revenue. Another line of attack has been that public service media is the product of the educated liberal elite, and is aimed squarely at people like themselves. In other words, it is asserted that the 'public' of the public service media is a liberal golem, with the consequence that content is shot through with a political bias designed to appeal to the sensibilities of a left wing media elite.

Even from the other flank, there are arguments against the ethos of US public service media that come from liberal and left wing commentators. Keane (1991: 125), for example, raises the possibility that public service media operates on the basis of an inherently contradictory set of funding arrangements. While acknowledging that an increasing proportion of the finance necessary to operate public service media comes from audience fees and donations, Keane joins with critics from the right in emphasizing the symbolic importance of that remaining portion of funding gathered from a combination of sponsors and non-profit organizations and, importantly, from the government, in the guise of the Corporation for Public Broadcasting. Regardless of how limited the financial support of government is, Keane points out, it comes loaded with a commitment to demonstrate 'objectivity and balance' in all programmes that may be thought of as controversial, and certainly throughout the news coverage (Corporation for Public Broadcasting 2005).

While a demand for objective standards sounds laudable enough on the face it, the place of objectivity in journalism is a contentious matter. In a well-known study of a New York newsroom – albeit one outside of the fold of public service – Gaye Tuchman (1972) finds that objectivity is defined mainly around the established professional practices of news selection and composition. In Tuchman's account, the practices associated with objectivity amount to a 'strategic ritual' that journalists and news organizations use to deflect criticism with the shield of established professional practices. The problematic result of these well worn practices of recognizing and reporting news is that 'although such procedures may provide demonstrable evidence of an attempt to obtain objectivity, they cannot be said to provide objectivity' (Tuchman 1972: 676). Furthermore, John Pilger (2006) argues that the attendant obligation to give space to two sides of a controversy fails to account for the likely unequal access to the resources of communication opposing sides in a news event normally enjoy, and prevents the journalist from engaging with the moral dimensions of the issues they are covering. For Pilger, objectivity is simply another one of the means by which journalists set about 'internalising the priorities and vocabulary of established power' (Pilger 2006: 1).

The obligation of objectivity in the context of public service media is important because of the scope it gives to those featuring in investigative news stories, especially, to complain about their treatment. More than anyone, it is those in legislative and economic power that can wield the weapon of 'due objectivity' against any public service outlet when news coverage becomes commercially or politically inconvenient. The wealthier or more connected they are, the louder they are able to complain. Therefore, while direct government interference is forbidden by the terms of the 1967 Act, the link between the future of this funding and the content of journalistic output discourages too harsh a focus on those in corporate or legislative power. In other words, Keane (1991) and Pilger (2006) point out, it might be argued that the funding arrangements that come with public service media militate against journalistic integrity.

Although these are subject to similar pressures around state funding, there are public service arrangements outside of the United States that see a more direct relationship between the state and media sectors, such that the discourse of public service has become embedded in large scale national media institutions (Keane 1991: 117). These arrangements can be found in Canada, Australia, Japan and much of Europe, and are mainly based on the 'public service broadcasting' model that was developed in the UK after the formation of the British Broadcasting Corporation (originally Company) in 1922. Unlike the US model, the majority of BBC funding comes from the state by means of a television licence fee, supplemented through the sale of BBC merchandise and international transmission rights. Peculiar to the BBC, an extra government grant is also awarded to maintain a 'World Service' arm that broadcasts select BBC radio output globally.

Although the BBC began life as a monopoly, the arrangement typified by the BBC should be distinguished from forms of state controlled broadcasting that currently exist in totalitarian states or those without fully developed media complexes. Rather than direct rule, the relationship between the broadcasters and the state in public service broadcasting is one of accountability for the level of service seen to be provided: an issue that is normally subject to periodic review. Themes shared through the various public models include common availability, the production of diverse content, programming specifically aimed at minority groups, insulation from the direct force of state or commercial interests, a focus on the quality of programming over audience figures and the provision of a creative environment for programme makers and journalists.

Just as important, however, is the financial relationship between public service broadcasters and the state. We have already noted that BBC funding is delivered by means of a fixed licence fee payable by all households with television receivers, and in the case of the Australian Broadcasting Corporation (ABC), funding is provided entirely by the state in the form of an ongoing system of government grants. While Australia does have another, smaller public service broadcaster – the Special Broadcasting Service (SBS) – that accepts a limited amount of sponsorship and advertising revenue, neither the main ABC nor the BBC takes money from commercial sponsors or advertising. Similar arrangements to those in the United Kingdom and Australia exist in the case of Sveriges television and radio in Sweden and NHK television and radio in Japan.

We have already looked at those arguments that the regulation of content – even when it is well intended – means that the force of public accountability interferes with the integrity of media professionals. Another key obligation of public service media which is potentially problematic has been to keep pace with, and where possible trail blaze, technological developments in media. Often this occurs within media sectors. In the UK, for example, the BBC has been instrumental in the promotion of digital radio, while Japan's national broadcaster NHK instigated and was the first to introduce high definition television. Although conceding that shifts to other media platforms are not always provided for within current legislation, Richard Naylor et al. (2000: 140) point to the relative success of the BBC in fashioning a presence on the Internet and extending their public remit online. Yet this was not a straightforward projection of public interest into new fields, and Naylor et al. argue that the early online ventures of the BBC offer a case study in the dilemmas between commercial forms of funding and those seen as appropriate to public service media. There was at first a limited amount of resolve on the part of the BBC to use the Internet, and in the mid-1990s this resulted in the establishment of the joint commercial venture, beeb.com, mixing 'shopping on the Web' with content derived from BBC television and radio. This commercially driven site was later to be branded far more explicitly as bbcshop.com. The much larger BBC Online website (bbc.co.uk) was launched relatively soon after with a remit more in keeping with a conventional public service obligation to educate, inform and entertain. Indeed, the quality of news coverage on BBC Online, coupled with the inbuilt capacity to link and archive events, is now a key element in how the BBC defines its success in performing its public role. Even online, though, public service has to be seen to be untroubled by commercial considerations, and Naylor et al. (2000: 143–4) point to broadly held misgivings at the juxtaposition of the commercial activity associated with a conventional Internet operation and the organizational commitment to public rather than consumer service. It is in the context of this need to demonstrate this commitment to a public rather than to a body of consumers that the most recent manifestation of bbcshop.com has continued to ensure that BBC Online is relatively insulated from commerce.

Public service media has therefore offered a prominent means by which a sector of the media industry can be seen to discharge any duty to the public, and through which various governments are able to show a commitment to harnessing communication technology towards the public good. However, increasingly the practice of public service media has become a matter for political dispute. The development of these arguments, allied with the socio-political circumstances of individual states, have resulted in a number of quite different models of public service across different states, from the public service media of the US to the public service broadcasting tradition of the UK. A number of key issues have predominated in these debates. From neo-liberal quarters public service media has been seen as an indulgent extension of state power. The arrangement provides a means by which the state can assert an approved form of publicness over all others. Others, particularly from the critical left, argue that the demand for 'neutrality' typically made of state supported media runs contrary to the conditions necessary for a brand of journalism with a clear idea of good and bad, and a determination to champion the side of the good. It is also worth noting that the range of resources and systems of accountability required to run a public service operation mean that not only is it confined to those countries willing to make the necessary investment, but also to those corporations such as the BBC in the UK, Länder broadcasting in Germany and the ABC in Australia. It is an inevitable outcome of this that public service media operates at the level of the state sponsored institution, and is therefore open to the accusation that it effectively operates at one step remove from the public that it seeks to serve.

Public service and governmentality

Key both to the conception and to the criticism of using media to serve the public interest is the necessity to influence the quality of the everyday practices of the population, at least in terms of media consumption. However, it is crucial to Foucault's conception of governance that power and control moves in different directions and to various ends, and is directed towards institutions as well as persons. This means that, while our focus so far has been on 'the public' as a means of collapsing localized concerns and interests into that of 'the population', we could equally look at the exercise of governmentality in and over media institutions themselves. David Nolan (2006), for example, looks on public service broadcasting as a means of governing media performance. His particular focus is on the Australian Broad-casting Corporation, and the terms according to which it was subject to regulatory criticism for its coverage of the 2003 Iraq conflict, although there are many parallels with the controversy that surrounded the BBC's coverage of the validity of the conflict that eventually gave rise to the Hutton Report, the circumstances and discursive consequences of which have been summarized by Martin Montgomery (2007: 130). According to Nolan (2006: 228) many of these difficulties to beset public service broadcasters stem from the peculiar idea of citizenship implicit in the terms of public service. This presents 'the public' as, on the one hand, the projected outcome of responsible and inf[...] practice, while at the same time providing the im[...] professional evaluation: effectively 'critical ideal [...] simultaneously'. In this formulation, the public [...] cause of high minded exasperation and problem [...] project in rectifying a constructed 'civic deficit' – [...] productive reading of the public as a complex of 'social relations and material practices' as they exist at present and prior to the elevated intervention of the paternalists. Unfortunately, according to Nolan (2006: 229), the former view of the ideal citizenry has come to dominate existing accounts of public service broadcasting, including that of Paddy Scannell (1992). Such narrow forms of public, as David Morley (2000) has also argued, fall within predictable ethnic, gendered and political boundaries, and so emerge as both reactionary and exclusionary.

The introduction of a Foucauldian view of governmentality to the problem of 'the public' in public service broadcasting offers a number of insights. It first of all alerts us to the role the vocabulary of public plays in defining and delimiting acceptable forms of citizenship. It also acknowledges that the practices of government operate across a number of social contexts – among the population as well as at the legislative level – and ultimately fashion the public they appear to serve. According to Nolan (2006: 233), public service broadcasting presents those legislative bodies a strategic means to exercise regulation and control by turning this constitutive relationship around, and so deploying the public as a weapon rather than an object of governance. This offers a critical perspective on recommendations by Denis McQuail (2003) and others for a professionalized media system, based on the introduction of systematized training and accountability procedures. It is Nolan's view that the constrained view of public that we see in public service broadcasting offers a ready means by which governance can be exercised simply by recourse to the supposed professionalism of the broadcasters in how they discharge their duties to this artificial 'public'. Two of the criteria for this public duty highlighted by Nolan are the avoidance of 'bias' and demonstration of 'objectivity'. The difficulties that both terms present with regards to both definition and practice have been discussed in detail by Michael Schudson (1995), but their implementation serves to remove from the journalist any claim to be 'public representative' (Higgins 2008), by demanding a curb on editorial comment and the continual recourse to outside sources with their own vested interests (Nolan 2006: 238). While we will return to Nolan's own recommendations later in the book, he sees 'public service' media as it stands as a tool of legislative control, rather than what it is supposed to be: a means to base the spread of governance on 'how various social practices and itutions contribute to formations of citizenship' at the level of veryday media practice and consumption. Public service, in other words, would do better to empower rather than to restrain those it pretends to serve.

Conclusion

Even at this early stage, it is clear that notions of 'the public' are a matter of some contention in the production of media, media policy and regulation, and media funding. 'The public', it seems, is a key term in the struggle over how best to assert a normative evaluation on what is problematically described as the 'media audience'. This chapter has shown that much of what is at stake in this battle concerns two possible options. One position perceives the media audience as those to whom the broadcasters have a professional duty of care and owe allegiance, whereas the other position sees any audience as a body of media consumers with the potential to consume much else, with any accountability to be served through the mechanisms of market forces. This first chapter has also shown the importance of vocabularies of the public in alerting us to the role of media as an instrument of 'governance'. That is, for good or ill, we are concerned with the role that media might have in fashioning the audience into a coherent and malleable citizenry.

This book is built on a division between political and cultural forms of public. The rationale behind this division will become clear as the chapters proceed but merits brief elaboration here. Politics we take to be activities of representative government and authority and the contribution, whether negative or positive, of citizens and others towards those activities. The political public is taken as those addressed in the role of their being either represented by those in or seeking government, or in the capacity of their being empowered with an electoral role in deciding that government. The key to this definition lies in its contrast with Colin Seymore-Ure's (1968: 284) notion of the 'political public', where he intends those politicians and civil servants charged with the formulation and implementation of policy. The political public we are concerned with are those to whom these political classes are, in principle at least, answerable. Membership of a public, as John Hartley (1996) suggests, is an issue of practice. (Hartley sees this as a practice of interpreting roles in the same way as one would seek to make sense of a text.) Those addressed as members of the political public at one minute might therefore find themselves addressed as members of another form of public the next; and the reverse is also true. All individuals in a democratic state will therefore routinely exercise their capacity to switch between the political and other forms of public. While this might betray some attachment to the exercise of democratic politics in particular, media genres that are not directly concerned with politics will be seen as belonging to the realm of the cultural public. In this, we follow Raymond Williams in taking a broad view of culture, while at the same time wishing to pursue Williams's insistence that culture has a political dimension. We will see that the politics of culture involves both the 'colonization' of other media forms by the concerns of government and the constant negotiation of social power and cultural/political strategies of definition. Part of the argument will be that it is the political dimension of culture that behoves us to separate out and demarcate its democratic function.

Questions for discussion

- Try and provide a definition of 'the public' in a way that avoids being overly judgemental and exclusionary, while at the same time providing a viable focus for the exercise of media policy.
- The link between public and governance attaches great significance to the conduct of everyday life. How might you attach notions of publicness to aspects of your daily conduct that initially appear apolitical and disconnected from broader social arrangements?

Further reading

Hannay, A. (2005) *On the Public*. Abingdon: Routledge.
Scannell, P. (1990) Public service broadcasting: the history of a concept, in A. Goodwin and G. Whannel (eds), *Understanding Television*. London: Routledge.
Warner, M. (2002) *Publics and Counterpublics*. New York: Zone.

2 The construction of the political public

Introduction

The purpose of this chapter is to look at how this idea of a political public has come to develop in its relationship with the institutions of media. Much of this discussion will centre on how the mediated political public has come to be portrayed through the construction of 'public opinion'. We will look critically at the development of public opinion as a shared concern of the institutions both of media and of politics, as well as at the industrialization of public opinion. We will then discuss the presentation of mass media as a forum for airing shared concerns; what Jürgen Habermas describes as 'the public sphere'. We will then go on to explore some of the terms of media as public sphere that will be developed more fully in later chapters, with an emphasis on how the public sphere can be used as a normative basis for examining media performance. We will also describe what is often seen as the colonization of the mediated public sphere by professional communicators and marketers, and offer some reflections on the implications of this for the integrity of the political public. We conclude with a discussion of the role media might play in the reconfiguration and empowerment of a political public: a formation of public that cultivates an informed and active citizenry.

Democracy, the public and the media

It would be just about impossible to conceive of a democratic state without some idea of what constitutes the public. The very term 'democracy' is generally taken to mean power by or on behalf of the populace. Even as a label of convenience (Lucas 1976: 9), the claim to be a champion or defender of democracy has proved a useful political tool across a number of historical contexts. If, as Churchill claimed, democracy is merely the 'least-worst' form of government, a saving grace might be that it is the easiest to marshal in political rhetoric. Even Charles Pigott's relentlessly cynical review of the political lexicon of the eighteenth century lauds the 'democrat' as one 'who maintains the rights of the people' (Pigott 1795: 14). These possibilities for speechifying are perhaps rarely as apparent as when the appellation of 'democracy' appears in its more outwardly perverse contexts – for example, in effective one-party states such as the former East Germany – where the surrounding political rhetoric is driven by talk of the maintenance of popular choice. Just as awkwardly, the winner-takes-all arrangements we see in the UK and in Australia routinely elect governments on a minority of votes (Arblaster 1987: 3), and while the situation is less common in the United States, it was just such a minority mandate that saw George W. Bush take the presidency of the United States in 2000. Yet, even in the complex manifestations of democracy that we currently see in such political contexts as the United States, Europe and Australia – the states with which we are primarily concerned in this book – notions of citizenry and the idea of popular participation, defined to different degrees, inform the communicative arrangements that drive the political process.

Yet, ideally, viable democracies also encourage political choice by cultivating orderly disagreement. So in order that they might fulfil their electoral role, the democratic public engage in periodic discussion about their alternatives for government, and the notion of 'deliberative democracy' has been developed to describe the productive capacity of this dispute (Elster 1998b). Furthermore, the terms of the deliberative democracy require that the lines of division are sustained or re-engaged even after the democratic act of voting has taken place and the views of the majority – or largest minority – have been seen to prevail. Political disagreement is therefore ongoing, so that the future electoral prospects of a government partly depend on continuing engagement with public discussion. Those uncertain mandates often bestowed by a winner-takes-all model of democratic representation are partly offset by an assumption of recurrent, productive dispute and resolution: a set of practices that also guard against what Alexis de Tocqueville ([1840] 1968) calls the 'tyranny of the majority' prevailing over duties of representation.

It seems, then, that the constructs of 'the people' that drive the democratic process are fragmented from the start, even if these divisions bring a political dynamism. By and large, electorates are divided into minorities of various magnitudes of significance that are driven by different motivations and material interests. Yet for all that, it is useful to have a means of describing these amorphous bodies of subjects in whose name democracies are formed and defended. Not least, this is because each citizen is considered to share material concerns with the people around them, and might be persuaded of another point of view on how best to pursue those collective interests. As Sennett (2002) notes, it is the joining of the formal responsibilities of citizenship with the culture and politics of everyday living that offers the lexicon of the public as a principle means by which a democratic people have come to be conceptualized. Drawing on a similar bank of meaning to those ideas of 'public service' media discussed in the last chapter, varying notions of public and publicness have become central to the manner in which media and civic authorities deal in politics (Rosen 1991: 204). Within this descriptive field, it is the public that files through the polling stations each time there is a state, regional or local election, occupying the temporary role of the active electorate. Also, what Habermas (1976) describes as the periodic 'legitimation crises' that beset liberal democracies are occasioned by perceived dips in public engagement with the given system of democratic representation. In sum, popular involvement remains a central component of the discourses that surround democratic politics and the public has become a dominant means of expressing this relationship between the citizenry and the government.

Ideas of the public, of public interest and of public representation, as well as to the conceptualization of politics itself, are also central to the way media engage in the political process. Many have sought to argue that media have a profound responsibility to help maintain a functioning democracy. Thomas Jefferson, made US President in 1801, contested the state censorship of rival John Adams by insisting that 'liberty depends on freedom of the press' (1946: 98), and a more recent discussion on television notes that 'the dynamics of democracy are intimately linked to the practices of communication, and [that] societal communication increasingly takes place within the mass media' (Dahlgren 1995: 2). Of course even where mass media output seems to meet this onerous responsibility, there are explanations other than a sense of democratic duty that help explain the dynamic between media and politics. Indeed, if we consider the key point of 'political economy' that media operate within the terms of a domineering financial and political framework (Mosco 1996), it seems likely that this relationship involves an implicit trade-off between media and the legislative might of the state. For all that, however, the forms of association to emerge are rarely outwardly venal. For example, we will recall from the last chapter that in the context of the United States, Australia and much of Europe, broadcast media output is licensed, and major sectors of media are required to meet particular standards of centrally defined public service, defined within the context of the governing interests of the state.

There is also an economic dimension to any media complicity with the dominant political arrangement. Indeed, it is this latter dimension that helps us to understand why the great majority of mass media that are not bound by an explicit public service remit nonetheless stay comparatively wedded to the democratic state. Vincent Mosco (1996), for example, attaches a particular significance to the predominance of a 'free market' approach to economic management, seeing this as key to understanding the operation of communications industries in post-industrial democracies. In a classic essay outlining a political economy of media, Peter Golding and Graham Murdock (1996) argue that industry and governmental collusion in the production of a consumption focused social environment has enabled major media corporations to generate considerable revenue in subscription and advertising, with only a significant minority relying upon direct government funding. While it is true that commercial success brings more creative scope (Downey 1996), the instinctive autonomy of even the most diligent media professional is therefore restricted by the oppressive realities of the economic landscape within which any industry is obliged to function (Golding and Murdock 1996: 23).

The construction of public opinion

Does careful use of public opinion offer a way of navigating this complex representation terrain? Karl Popper ([1954] 1992: 154) remarks that 'owing to its anonymity, public opinion is an irresponsible form of power'. Of 'calls to the people' in general, Margaret Canovan (1981: 261) notes that 'while providing a fine rallying cry [they are] singularly lacking in precise meaning'. Indeed, it is arguably this very ambiguity that gives the testament on the basis of the collective its political force. Michel Pêcheux (1988) portrays the claim to popular support and sentiment as a 'discursive struggle' for the prize of naming political events and making them emblematic of some greater political cause. It is important to stress that such claims can be quite fanciful. While Gabriel Tarde warns of the prominence that emotionality assumes over material interests (Katz 2006: 267), the full extent of this creative latitude becomes apparent in a study by Elliot King and Michael Schudson (1995) that describes how the one sided portrayal of 'public opinion' that surrounded the early years of the Ronald Reagan presidency with the glow of popularity flew directly in the face of more compelling evidence of widespread public contempt.

Given this importance attached to comprehending the public mind, it is hardly surprising that the art of discerning and reporting upon the views of the political public has generated a medium sized industry. Although unsystematic 'straw polls' have been published since the *Harrisburg Pennsylvanian* predicted the presidential election of 1824 (Moon 1999: 6), the 1930s saw the beginnings of a sector dedicated to more systematic polling. While there are many substantial players such as MORI in the UK, perhaps the best known member of this sector is the Gallup polling organization, founded in 1935 in admirable pursuit of 'the pulse of democracy' (Gallup 1940), and who distinguished themselves from the polls of the day by applying 'scientific sampling' methods toward establishing public opinion (Rogers 1949: 101; Fishkin 1997: 78). Gallup currently has 27 offices worldwide, including branches in the US, Australia, China and several European countries. In addition to such specialist agencies as Gallup and MORI there are also various businesses and departments, from the retail sector to academic and government departments, routinely engaged in gathering and analysing public opinion to various ends and priorities, ranging from consumer trends to health and crime surveys (Miller 1995: 112). It has partly been in order to respond to and encourage discussion of this industry that the learned journal *Public Opinion Quarterly* began publication just two years after the foundation of Gallup. The measurement of public opinion has also become an important aspect of the business of politics beyond the nation state. Latterly, having constant access to polls of public opinion has become so important to the European Commission, for example, that it runs an in-house Public Opinion Analysis sector.

Yet, in spite of the firm establishment of public opinion in the political realm, we should be wary of supposing that there was ever a moment when the notion was given universally uncritical treatment. Even in the nineteenth century, William Hazlitt (1991: 144) dismissed public opinion as seeking to pass off the volume of the chorus as articulacy of expression. But when we look to those writings in which the conceptual legitimacy of public opinion is assumed, it is often easy to see the prejudices that lie behind. Writing at the outset of the twentieth century, James Bryce ([1900] 1966) outlined what he sees as the stages in the development of public opinion, starting 'when a sentiment spontaneously rises in the mind and flows from the lips of the average man', through further discussion in the 'counting house' with business partners and aided by a 'bundle of further newspapers', before a journalist 'whose business it is to discover what people are thinking' gathers where the day's deliberations have led, and incorporates this, together with their own thoughts, into the next day's papers.

Although a product of its 1900 vintage, the assumptions of gender and social class in Bryce's account are clear: the member of the public is male and holds a senior position in business. There is also an assumption that representative members of the public live in New York or some other financial centre, and certainly in an urban environment. What is equally significant, though, is that driving force of public opinion is neither the gut reaction at the breakfast table nor deliberation among colleagues, but the views and agendas of media. Even in Bryce's largely speculative view, opinion formation is punctuated by consultation with the newspapers of the day, and takes a more developed form on the newsstands of the following morning. What is also apparent from Bryce's account is that the use and manipulation of public opinion is one of the means by which media organizations establish a rapport with what they see as their audience. According to Bryce, it is the job of the journalist to track the mood of public discussion so that the newspaper as accurately as possible reflects the readership's views back to itself.

In his book *Public Opinion,* first published in 1922, Walter Lippmann ([1922] 1997) expresses a concern with what he saw as the misuse of this allusion to a collective consciousness and how it has come to be incorporated into the conduct of media. As well as offering the first book length study of the phenomenon of public opinion, Lippmann is also still widely referenced for his hostility towards 'mass society' and his view that such an arrangement, in William Kornhauser's (1960: 27) words, 'produces rule by the incompetent'. Lippmann begins his attack by suggesting that individuals construct their own 'realities' on the basis of their immediate environment. This has the fearful consequence that individual perceptions emerge replete with parochial self-interest and social prejudice. Lippmann argues that this has infected the media industries, where workers incorporate an idea of public opinion into their everyday practice by pandering to the dispositions of the target readership, which in turn replenishes the very well from which this tawdry mindset is drawn ([1922] 1997: 215).

There are ways in which Lippmann's analysis was problematic even for its time; for example, he dismisses the idea that the popular notion of self-interest may conceal approaches to the economy and social class (Lippmann [1922] 1997: 119). But if *Public Opinion* was to be controversial, still more contentious was Lippmann's ([1927] 1993) suggestion in the later *The Phantom Public* that an intellectual elite step in to take the place of these incompetent masses, provoking the ire of John Dewey (1929) among others. Yet while his cure is an unlikely one, Lippmann's lasting contribution has been his diagnosis that 'public opinion' is an insidious conceit that weighs on media practice. According to Lippmann, even the most independently minded newspaper journalist is constrained by the futile and politically hazardous responsibility of pinning down, speaking to, and helping to form public opinion:

> If the newspapers, then, are to be charged with the duty of translating the whole public life of mankind, so that every adult can arrive at an opinion on every moot topic ... they are bound to fail. It is not possible to assume that a world, carried on by a

division of labour and distribution of authority, can be governed by universal opinions in the whole population. Unconsciously the theory sets up the reader as omnicompetent, and puts upon the press the burden of accomplishing what representative government, industrial organization, and diplomacy have failed to accomplish

(Lippmann [1922] 1997: 228)

While instinctively mistrustful of the institutions of media, Lippmann expresses his regret that media's contribution to activities of state, law and governance is curtailed by a commitment to a confected public opinion (Lippmann [1922] 1997: 229). Albeit that it is bound up with his intrinsic mistrust of 'the masses', Lippmann would prefer that the press cast off the shackles of popular representation and become agents of information and intelligence. Where Pierre Bourdieu (1979: 129) differs is in his desire that a truly popular and diverse form of politics should predominate over a system of practice that presents the public mind as one. Whereas Lippmann accuses public opinion of distracting the competent deliberations of the political elite, Bourdieu sees it as an establishment tool to dismiss the masses in an easy and sweeping definition.

If anything, however, the use of public opinion in media has become more wilful in its focus on the priorities of political elites. In his book *Constructing Public Opinion*, Justin Lewis (2001) highlights what he sees as an exercise in complicity between the dominant media and political institutions. While many of Lewis's objections are against the methods that opinion pollsters employ, they are nevertheless consequential in terms of their outcome. According to Lewis, the practice of public opinion research bespeaks an assumption that the social and political environment can be expressed in terms of statistical and numerical data. He argues that the rendering of social phenomenon in this way denies context and imposes a 'meaning' decided, in the main, by those in a position to decide upon what survey questions are the best ones to be asked and what descriptive categories ought to be invoked. The outcomes of public opinion surveys are therefore politically and culturally loaded and simplistic in their assessment of citizen engagement.

Of course, as Lewis acknowledges, these are mere scholarly distinctions for a journalist with a story to compose. At least in principle, well produced polls should make governments more democratic (Lavrakas and Traugott 2000: 321). And, as Patterson (2005) points out, the creative use of popularity polls allow the often complex debates around political administration to be recast as an equestrian steeplechase, complete with outside bets, steady runners, spectacular falls and home-stretch dashes. Admittedly, a number of public service media outlets such as the BBC issue guidelines on the prominence that should be accorded to opinion polls, and the context in which they should be placed (Brookes et al. 2004: 65). In general terms, though, polls and surveys are central to the daily work practices of the journalist to the extent that in an effort to combat some of the most badly informed readings, the American Newspaper Publishers Association has commissioned and subsequently reprinted a book dedicated to the interpretation of polls and surveys in a newsroom environment (Wilhoit and Weaver [1980] 1990).

In advising a cultivated wariness towards the compositional practices of public opinion, Lewis taps into a long-standing concern in media scholarship around the means by which 'representative' population samples are gathered, coupled with the political and cultural implications of flawed sampling methods. Analysis of the production of US television viewing figures finds audience totals based on the viewing activities of those households with a ratings meter installed, or those that happen to subscribe to cable television (Meehan 1990). The outcome of such surveys are what can best be described as packets of 'audience', produced solely to provide a measurable commodity for media institutions to sell to advertisers (Meehan 1990: 132; Ang 1991: 53). While in Lewis's account, the strategies of opinion pollsters are similarly motivated towards the production of commodity statistics, the issues of 'inclusion and exclusion' from the public survey are bound up with the issues of population and governance discussed in the last chapter. By way of example, Lewis (2001: 27) points to the work of Lipari, who shows how questions around such issues as welfare and immigration are phrased in a manner that assumes respondent *concern* about welfare and immigration policies, rather than that a respondent may *be subject to* such policies. In terms of how the sample is then subject to interpretation, Virginia Sapiro (2002) argues that opinion polls routinely downplay the influence of gender in opinion formation, such that divisions in public opinion that are expressed in terms of a population split could be more accurately conveyed as a gendered distribution.

Yet, in spite of the limited field of expression, the findings of opinion polls often reveal more liberal and left-of-centre views than much of media is accustomed to reporting (Lewis 2001: 44). Jeffrey Scheuer (2001: 126) describes a context in which the instinct for self-interest and retribution advocated by the political right fits more readily with soundbite driven forms of media presentation, than the relatively complex communitarian and interventionist policies of the political left. Against this background, any aberrant results of surveys tend to be manipulated, to be used selectively or to be framed in such a way that they fit within an established media agenda. Or results may be ignored altogether. Lewis (2001: 47) notes that feedback from opinion surveys is dismissed as irrelevant if it does not fit within what media see as the prevailing political realities, such as 'serious' political candidates and institutions. Overall, Lewis argues, the outcomes of opinion polls are expected to portray an orderly political public focused on dominant issues and willing to occupy a reasonable and pragmatic position in any debate (Lewis 2001: 56-7). As Bourdieu (1979) points out, a topic's status as a matter of 'public interest' is a necessary condition of the opinion poll that positions it as so, meaning that polls contribute to what Maxwell McCombs (1994) calls an 'agenda setting' function, by asserting certain topics over others, thereby producing a self-fulfilling representation of public opinion. On those occasions where polls yield opinion contrary to the dominant political frame – such as was the case in the UK's participation in the 2001 invasion of Iraq – Lewis (2001: 55) insists that media organizations sympathetic to the government line routinely exercise the option of disregarding such results as 'ignorant or confused'.

However, Brookes et al. (2004) suggest that even having no suitable opinion poll to hand does not discourage political journalists from making reference to what the public are thinking on a given matter. When a suitable opinion poll does present itself, Brookes et al. (2004: 70) find that polls are referred to when they suit the dominant frame of the coverage. However, Brookes et al. also show how discourses of public opinion infiltrate news discourse through mere inference, ably illustrated by the unsubstantiated claim made by a BBC journalist that 'there are a very large number of people in this country who want to leave the European Union' (in Brookes et al. 2004: 71-2). Such conjectures, Brookes et al. argue, tend to follow one of two politically motivated patterns: either the public would be said to be disenchanted with aspects of the electoral process, a mood conveniently in keeping with a media narrative of electoral disillusion that runs through coverage more generally, or speculations on public opinion would see it sharing the concerns of the main political parties (Brookes et al. 2004: 72). As we go on to look at how we might best conceptualize media's relationship with the political public, it is therefore worth bearing in mind that the expression of the political public operates as a politically interested form of representation.

The media as a public sphere

Jürgen Habermas's notion of 'the public sphere' has emerged as one of the most widely used means of establishing the place of the contemporary political public and its processes of opinion formation, especially in terms of the contribution of media (Dahlgren 1995). The public sphere emerges from a view of politics as a process of dialogue, and is meant to describe a platform for negotiating and reconciling competing interests, so that the formation of public policy is aided by the informed intervention of concerned citizens. In Habermas's account, the original public sphere was conceived in the coffee and chocolate houses that emerged in mid-seventeenth century London. There, an informal mix of the aristocratic and merchant classes would gather together to throw themselves good heartedly into caffeine charged 'economic and political disputes' (Habermas 1989: 32–3). In its ideal formation, arguments would triumph or flounder on their own strengths rather than on the standing of the individual concerned. Thus, a routine practice of productive dispute was set in place that will see the most compelling arguments prevail, and through which 'something approaching public opinion can be formed' (Habermas 1979: 198). While the coffee shops present the public sphere in a form that has been subject to decay ever since, Habermas (1979: 198) notes that in the contemporary circumstances of mass suffrage, 'newspapers and magazines, radio and television are the media of the public sphere'.

Of course, there is more to popular empowerment and the triumph of political reason than opening a selection of coffee shops or even the establishment of a media empire. So what else needs to be in place for a public sphere to develop? According to Habermas, it depends upon the formation of an organized and relatively coherent body of government; in other words, a 'knowable' civic authority that the participants within the sphere may judge and hold to account. It is also predicated on any productive disputation obtaining between rationally minded individual citizens, who are subject to but remain relatively independent of these governing authorities. In addition, however limited this capacity may in effect be, the participants of any public sphere should have the means to communicate their views to the governing authorities. As we will see in Chapters 3 and 4, this arrangement between citizens and government is often built into media discourse on politics. The government may well have representative voices there to contribute to the debate, but the core of the gathering still has to be composed of interested citizens of varying types. Lastly, as Charles Taylor (1995: 264–5) points out, it is vital that the public sphere be understood as a place for discussion and not for organizing the act of voting or the instigation of political policy, insisting 'it is supposed to be listened to by those in power, but is not in itself an exercise of power'.

Habermas's original conception of the public sphere has been subject to a great deal of constructive criticism, and Habermas himself has acknowledged both its dependence upon an idealized historical arrangement and its limited definition of constructive citizenship (Habermas 1992). However, in order to make the most of Habermas's account, we should interpret the public sphere as an ideal against which normative assessments may be made of media or political performance; what Peter Dahlgren (1991: 5) describes as a 'model' or a 'vision' of the potential of the media/politics arrangement.

Even so, the dimensions of this discursive space still need to be established. One interpretation of the relationship between a public sphere and political authority is that discussion circulates beyond the physical environment of any specific gathering point, and extends to the 'boundaries of democratic action' within which the competent governing forces are elected and exercise control (Higgins 2006: 27). Garnham (1992) and Higgins (2006) insist this should default to the level of state – where much policy control resides – but depending on the circumstances these discursive boundaries may be adjusted to include local or global spaces of representative government. Stepping aside from this commitment to governmental space, Meryl Aldridge (2007: 19) points to Habermas's (1996) later emphasis on the place of 'organized groups' in generating of public discussion, many pursuing political interests outside of the state framework. While Aldridge's concern is with the local, her emphasis on social networks also alerts us to the possibility of international public spheres around issues such as climate change. Certainly, these would be in keeping with Clive Barnett's (2003) argument, one we will look at in more detail in Chapter 8, that the point of mediated public spheres are their transcendence of traditional boundaries.

However, while the idea of a commonly accessible public sphere implies some degree of common interest among the participants, with disagreement on how those interests are to be realized, there remains a need to be mindful of those separate realms of political action whose aims and beliefs are in opposition to one another (Habermas 1992). For example, we can identify competing public spheres by their position in the economic system, gender, physical ability, sexual preference, religious affiliation or any of a number of other politically informed modes of belonging, and find that in interactive terms many of these competing realms are likely to be irreconcilable. That is, while the possibilities offered by the public sphere stem from the clash of ideas, the need for a multiplicity of public spheres stem from differences in interests and priorities (Warner 2002).

The marketization of the political public

There are still other emergent factors that may strike at the discursive basis on which the public sphere operates. As Habermas repeatedly points out, any public sphere remains in danger of malignant 'colonization' by non-rational forces of political engagement. We have already looked at the construction of public opinion, and at how this has spawned an industry of manipulation. But there are other communicative professions that may be said to offer a threat to the integrity of the public sphere, in that they are in the business of mobilizing resources to ensure that some political arguments have a greater prominence in any public realm than others. Both Aeron Davis (2002) and David Miller (2002) chart the rise of an international public relations industry and look critically at the investment the PR sector makes in order to position itself as the main conduit for political interest groups to access media and thence the public. Philip Howard (2006: 135), moreover, argues that a set of publicity industry practices have become internalised by a political establishment more interested in specific, targetable 'issue publics' than with the public at large. According to Leon Mayhew (1997: 209), PR agencies and specialist lobbying firms have taken such a hold in the United States that political advisers are transformed into information managers.

Indeed, this is just one part of Mayhew's broader thesis that the political realm is only one component of the cultivation of a 'new public' that operates as the subject, not of rational arguments for discussion, but for an increasingly sophisticated industry for the generation and satisfaction of consumer needs. Margaret Scammell (2003) and Heather Savigny (2008) track the emergence of the 'citizen consumer' through the imposition of a marketing model on political discourse. In this marketing model, the political public are cast as an aggregate of desires; producers of needs, which political policy can be designed to satisfy. As both Scammell and Savigny argue, this renders the public as customers of rather than participants in the political process: quite contrary to what Scammell (2003: 134) describes as 'the engaged and debating public'. The introduction of business principles to politics also assesses priorities in a way that emphasizes immediate returns – in terms of measurable goals – over longer term consequences. An especially insidious example of this occurs in US elections, where less politically viable constituencies and communities are 'redlined' from campaigns, and purposively excluded from receiving political information (Howard 2006: 131).

For Bob Franklin (2004), this emphasis on the political public as a body of consumers forms part of a wider diminution in the quality of public discourse on politics. Where media should be seeking to ensure the free circulation of politically significant information and policy ideas, an alliance of convenience between the political and media establishments have come to be concerned in only 'packaging politics' in a way that emphasizes attractiveness over genuine substance. According to Neil Postman (1987: 129), if satisfying 'the market' is at the core of public discourse then 'the idea is not to pursue excellence, clarity or honesty but to appear as though you are, which is another matter altogether'. There is, of course, a set of smaller scale alternative media outlets to call upon (Atton 2002), but as Leif Dahlberg (2006: 49) points out the quality of public debate becomes more of a problem the larger and more successful the major media corporations become – with the dominant consumerism discourse occupying 'proportionally more media space' and leaving the disempowered public to 'choose between the products'.

While this book is concentrated on broadcast media, Brian McNair (2006) emphasizes the capacity for public empowerment found in new media technologies such as online discussion forums and blogging. In an early assessment of the impact of the Internet on the democratic process, Mark Poster (1997) describes interested citizens exchanging views in virtual rather than physical environments. Peter Dahlgren and Tobias Olsson (2007) suggest that this produces a form of political engagement that realigns activities of citizenship with everyday practice and situates them within the domestic space. McNair (2006) argues that this proliferation of technology and its extension into private spaces undermines a 'control paradigm' approach that sees power as the preserve of media institutions. Such technologies provide the means, McNair argues, for media consumers to re-invigorate their credentials as citizens, initiate discussion on their own terms and according to their own agendas, and write and distribute their own journalistic content (McNair 2006: 121). This takes place within limits, of course, and using the metaphor of a 'walled garden', Livingstone (2005a: 174) points out that websites are designed with control in mind. Expression is subject to approval and censure, even if by the Internet service provider (ISP). Advertising is designed to be obtrusive, and software and content is designed to contain the user within one site. Furthermore, in an examination of how the Internet has been used every bit as effectively by the political establishment, Howard (2006: 3) describes the use of digital technology in 'hypermedia' political campaigns to regulate the distribution of political intelligence among the electorate, strengthening the boundaries of information poverty McNair (2006) insists are being breached.

The key, for Lewis et al. (2005), is to develop forms of media discourse that will help to re-engage the various media industries as more effective democratic actors. There are already a number of such discourses in place, they argue. In addition to the productive use of new media technologies highlighted by McNair (2006) and Dahlgren and Olsson (2007), such longer established strategies as the *vox pop* (where members of the public are interviewed as 'representative' voices) engages the citizen in a mode of direct address. What Lewis et al. (2005) advocate is a re-invigoration of the ordinary citizen as an active member of a political public through the development of a democratic ethic in media. Against this, it is necessary to weigh the evidence that such developments are often contrary to the instincts of the political establishment behind the current, unsatisfactory arrangement, who might be keen to maintain an emphasis on the ephemeral and populist over the pursuit of social justice and political principle. While the media should provide an environment in which the public sphere is populated by politically empowered citizens, what is needed are media willing to make efforts to inform as well as titillate their publics.

Conclusion

The precise nature of the concept of the public sphere has been critically examined from several quarters, and we have looked at a number of those contending that it has become a mere platform for consumer activity, in a way that diminishes the quality of political culture generally (Postman 1987; Franklin 2004). The suggestion has been that the public sphere can be usefully read as a normative category, offering an ideal arrangement against which to assess the political conduct of media (Higgins 2006). However, we have also acknowledged that different formations of public gather around divergent sets of interests, and that various configurations of public sphere emerge to accommodate these differences. A public gathering wishing to talk about taxation, for example, is likely to be one with an average income and weekly spend of a level that makes the amount of tax paid a real and present concern. Another gathering of people will wish to assess the best ways to combat racial harassment, and others will have shared interests attendant with the politics of sexual identification (Warner 2002). It may be that the original conception of the public sphere emphasizes elite publics deliberating on the relative worth of mainstream political ideologies, but later developments stress a multiplicity of competing public spheres, media forms and modes of engagement (Habermas 1992: 425). It is also noteworthy that these competing public spheres may draw upon sub-national networks and interest groups (Habermas 1996), the capacity of alternative media (Atton 2002), and capacity of the Internet towards offering new forms of mediated publicness (McNair 2006).

Questions for discussion

- Look over the previous month's media, and pick out two issues of 'public concern' that have figured in political coverage. Critically discuss any social, political or exclusionary agendas behind these expressions of shared concern and, where you can, examine whether they are based on public opinion research or whether they come from another source.
- Should there be more to the political public than our relationship with the democratic process? How much should we consider politically marginalized publics and to what degree should their preferences be taken into account in the media?

Further reading

Habermas, J. (1992) Further reflections on the public sphere, in C. Calhoun (ed.), *Habermas and the Public Sphere*. Cambridge, MA: MIT Press.
Keane, J. (1991) *The Media and Democracy*. Cambridge: Polity Press.
Lewis, J. (2001) *Constructing Public Opinion*. New York: Columbia University Press.

3 The political public and its advocates

Introduction

Now that we have gone over some of the issues surrounding the construction of the political public, this chapter will be the first of two to deal with ways in which the political public is integral to mass media. The focus in this chapter will be on how media presents itself as acting on behalf of this formation of public – that is, how media offers a claim to public advocacy. In order to do this, we will begin by looking at the roots of the idea of media as bearers of responsibility for the political public, and will suggest that configurations of public emerge to accommodate different media discourses. First, we will look at the discourse of the media professional as a public inquisitor, and how forms of populism are deployed in strategies of representation. We will then look at the emerging role of the entertainment talk show as a forum of political discussion, and reflect upon its potential as a form of media advocacy. Our main task throughout the chapter will be to assess the political and cultural implications of these developments in the political public.

The media and political responsibility

In his classic assessment of the modern capitalist state, Ralph Miliband (1973: 198) emphasizes the central role of the means of mass communication, and the relative strength of the larger circulation newspapers and broadcast organizations. James Curran and Jean Seaton acknowledge the occasional unease the political classes feel at this apparent media dominance. The title of their book on mass media draws upon the words of UK prime minister of the 1920s Stanley Baldwin that media institutions are in danger of exercising 'power without responsibility' (Curran and Seaton 1997: 42). Yet even with this uncertainty, the last chapter described a broad expectation that media will play a significant part promoting and communicating political arguments and the political process. As to how we should reflect upon and discuss this relationship, Jay Blumler and Michael Gurevitch (1995: 89) outline at least two approaches. On the one hand, they argue there is a 'pragmatic' assumption in place that while politics should ideally form part of media's concern with news, the level of coverage will inevitably depend on how newsworthy the current political stories or events happen to appear. From this perspective, levels of coverage will be both generated and limited by existent news values (Brighton and Foy 2007).

In contrast, Blumler and Gurevitch point to what they term the 'sacerdotal' assumption that media has an unstinting obligation to cover politics for its inherent importance, regardless of whether the political stories of the day happen to accord with the routines of news production. This latter approach is driven by a historically driven view of media, and the press in particular, as the 'Fourth Estate'. This expression is a complex and historically resonant one. It began as a pithy addition to the first three official estates of UK government, outlined by William Stubbs (1874: 583) as the clergy (the 'Lords Spiritual'), peers of the realm (the 'Lords Temporal'), and elected members of parliament (the 'Commons'). The fourth of these is the determinedly unofficial estate of popular power beheld by Thomas Carlyle, when he writes: 'In the Reporters' Gallery yonder, there sat a *Fourth Estate* more important far than they all. It is not a figure of speech, or a witty saying; it is a literal fact' (Carlyle 1840: 194). Thus, from the middle of the nineteenth century, the Fourth Estate has offered a pointed metaphor for the supposed transfer of power from the three traditional estates to media institutions, leaving media with the whip hand.

While Carlyle and his contemporaries accord the communication industries with an improbable amount of direct power, their view nonetheless establishes a tradition of presenting media as a public watchdog, with the speed, strength and ferocity to defend the greater civic good. Such ways of embodying media as the Fourth Estate or public watchdog lend themselves easily to mythologization, of course. Robert Entman (1989) makes just this point in his discussion of mass media in the United States: a state system in which the right to freedom of expression is written into the national constitutional. While the US system should be one in which media are unfettered, Entman argues that this freedom rarely moves beyond the symbolic level, and is curtailed by more powerful, and state approved religious and economic interests. According to Entman, we should be wary of the *performance* of a publicly accountable media taking precedence over its exercise of genuine influence (Entman 1989).

Yet for all the evidence to the contrary, the image of the reporter in particular as the defender of the interests of the democratic public remains a popular and comforting one. The figures of television journalist Edward R. Murrow and *Washington Post* reporters Woodward and Bernstein have provided exemplars for those keen to see media as guardians of freedom and democracy. Murrow used the platform of his CBS programme *See it Now* to expose renegade Senator Joseph McCarthy during the communist witch-hunts of the early 1950s, deploying a form of advocacy that, in a pattern that we will discuss in more detail later, calls upon the charisma of the individual media performer (Barnouw 1975: 172–84). Distinguishable by his throaty, crisp pronunciation, well groomed appearance and cigarette, Murrow provides what Barthes (1972) would call a contemporary 'mythology' of 1950s style demeanour mixed with old style American integrity. Edward R. Murrow embodies what Fredric Jameson (1991: 281) describes as the re-invention of the 1950s as a reservoir of nostalgia. This myth is fuelled by the subsequent narrativization of Murrow's difficult relationship with the corporate interests, which are presented as characteristically seeking to constrain honest journalism (Schudson 1995: 6). As if to demonstrate the internalization of these mythologies in US media history, both the Murrow and *Washington Post* episodes have become the subject of Hollywood movies in which the reporters have assumed the *dramatis personae* of defenders of the public good. Woodward and Bernstein's role in the Watergate exposure was portrayed in the Alan Pakula directed *All the President's Men* (1976), while Murrow's attack on the chicanery of McCarthy was the subject of a George Clooney directed film, *Good Night and Good Luck* (2006), using Murrow's ritual sign-off as its title.

Media and politics: the advocacy role

It therefore seems that national political well-being is in part determined by the seeming capacity and apparent willingness of mass media to operate with a sense of democratic responsibility. This and the following sections will now look at a number of the ways in which media are seen to represent the political public. In the provision of political coverage, there are two main directions from which the political public may be involved. One is for media to act on behalf of the public, and the other is for media to establish an arrangement in which the public have input. It is the first of these that the present chapter will be concerned with – what may be described as an 'advocacy role' for media. As its legalistic connotations would suggest, the advocacy approach figuratively positions media as the holders of a brief from the political public, and therefore professionally engaged on the public's behalf. So rather than untrained and haphazardly informed members of the general political public quizzing and investigating those in authority, such duties fall to those media professionals deemed to have the appropriate skills and personal bearing. The advocacy approach also means that the resources of the media institution work for the public good: including pools of trained investigators, reporters, questioners and archivists, all bringing official access to political and institutional circles through such arrangements as press passes and 'political lobby' memberships. Of course, dealt with uncritically, this notion of political advocacy invests a bond of trust in media institutions, against the advice of Bourdieu (1998), Entman (1989) and many others that much the of media is complicit in the suffocation of substantive political debate. At the very least, it is therefore necessary to include alternative and activist media outlets as a counter to the shortcomings in the performance of mainstream media (Atton 2002; Waltz 2005), and to heed the constant appraisal and criticism of more diligent journalists and academics (Miller 1993). Nonetheless, thinking of media as potential public advocate provides a means of conceptualizing its political capacity of media, as well as providing a normative ideal against which media may be subject to assessment and critique.

The form of public representation that concerns us in this chapter is where media appear to discharge this duty through the individual media professional. We have seen this through the focus of the history of a campaigning media on such mythical figures as Murrow. In our context, this media professional is presented as a specifically adept and well informed journalist who accepts and learns a set of instructions on an issue of public concern or public interest, and who then questions and probes those in power on the public's behalf. Montgomery (2007: 148) describes the encounters between these inquisitors and politicians as 'the accountability interview'. The parallels we draw between this position and that of a lawyer or public prosecutor are fruitful ones. In common with a lawyer in a courtroom setting, the trained journalist will be empowered to decide upon questions to which the public are entitled to receive an answer, and will pursue those questions irrespective whether the person being questioned desires transparency or not.

The public inquisitor

The position of what we can call the 'public inquisitor' and the discursive strategies associated with it have developed along with the apparatus of the broadcast media, and has always generated controversy (Higgins 2008). In the case of UK television, this form of public representation began to find full form in the 1950s when Robin Day. Day's first major interview with a prominent UK politician was conducted with prime minister Harold Macmillan for the ITN series *Tell the People* on 23 February 1958 (Day 1993: 21–30; Cockerell 1989: 62). In an account of the interview written in the early 1990s, Day concedes that by contemporary standards, his attitude to the prime minister was gentle to the point of old fashioned deference (Day 1993: 21). Even so, Day notes the predictable disquiet of the establishment figures of the press – the London-based *Daily Mirror* observed that 'the idiot's lantern is getting too big for its ugly gleam' – but in the fuller account offered by his memoirs, Day recalls that the prime minister himself saw an emerging shift in the dynamic between the politician and the professional interviewer:

> As we waited to begin, the Prime Minister derived considerable amusement from the seating arrangements. He dryly complained that he was sitting on a hard upright seat, whereas I was enthroned behind the table in a comfortable swivel chair with well-padded arms. This, said the Prime Minister, 'seemed to symbolize the new relationship between politician and TV interviewer'. He felt as if he was 'on the mat'. I offered to change chairs, but the Prime Minister, keeping up the banter, said, 'No, no. I know my place'.
>
> (Day 1989: 1)

Some more substantial problems were raised though. Aside from the temerity of Day in setting out the studio and asking the questions as he did, a number of newspapers editorials objected that this style of questioning might force the prime minster to formulate policy on the spot, so undermining both the cabinet and the essential procedures of due process (Day 1989: 4). In addition, such interviews place the prime minister in circumstances where he or she has to defend current government policy, which as events move from day to day, might mean having to defend the indefensible and then back up their spluttered answers with ill conceived actions. As the *Daily Mirror* again noted, Day asked Macmillan about the performance of a cabinet member that collegial courtesy would compel him to defend, thereby placing the prime minister in the anomalous position of having to back this support with the retention of 'a colleague who is obviously a disaster to British foreign policy' (Day 1993: 22). In essence, many of the objections to these interviews therefore proceed on the basis that public accountability should only be exercised at appropriate stages of the political process, and with the assumption that it is the instinct of media to overplay what they see as their public duty to the detriment of effective government.

Across national contexts, the development of this form of media advocacy has met with resistance. It is only after the media environment established by Walter Cronkite, Robin Day and others that the discursive arrangement of public advocacy made permissible questions that might otherwise have been seen as impertinent, an arrangement that, as Day (1989: 104) was later to observe, was 'fought for interview by interview'. This form of advocacy engendered a performed hostility that has come to be associated with diligent journalism. Reflecting these emergent practices of public representativeness, Robin Day was occasionally called upon to remind offended interviewees that his questions did not betray his own views, but merely reflected his duty to the most sceptical members of his public. As this form of political interview has become the norm, the interviewer has taken on the status and responsibility of what McNair (2000: 84) calls 'the licensed interrogator of the powerful'.

Steven Clayman (2002) is interested in how the most aggressive and contentious forms of these interviews maintain legitimacy, arguing that this stems from the interviewers' position as 'tribunes of the people'. Clayman (2002: 200) shows how interviewers such as Ted Koppel diffuse their own agency in the delivery of hostile questions by aligning them with various forms of the political public, be this through an appeal to 'the people' or 'the American people'. Also, on those occasions on which the interviewee expresses doubt over the propriety of a question or the legitimacy of an encounter, recourse to their role as public representative also forms part of the interviewers' rebuttal strategy, such that they claim merely to be harbinger of 'what the people are suggesting' (Clayman 2002: 208). Thus, according to Clayman (2002: 197), 'the role of public servant ... continues to have salience today, not only as a normative ideal that journalists strive for, but also as a strategic legitimating resource'.

The essential 'star' qualities of public inquisitors, as foremost defenders of public interest and legitimacy, mean they are necessarily limited in number at any given time. The United States has a history of such licensed interrogators, and Walter Cronkite, Barbara Walters, Ted Koppel and Dan Rather have been among the most notable. Current such advocates in the UK include Kirsty Wark, John Humphrys and Jeremy Paxman, all from the BBC, while Australia's roster includes Laurie Oakes of Channel Nine and Liz Jackson of the Australian Broadcasting Corporation. In the US, the various networks providing news coverage have promoted both their own news and current affairs programmes and their own star interviewers, of which the longest established and one of the most prominent is the NBC programme *Meet the Press*. This began in 1945 as a radio programme, and moved to NBC television two years later. Since the early 1990s, the presenter and interviewer on the *Meet the Press* has been Tim Russert, who also performs a similar role for *The Tim Russert Show* on CNBC. *Meet the Press* is publicized by NBC as their provision of a regular platform for interviews with important political figures of the day. There are echoes of Carlyle's comments on the Fourth Estate in NBC's (2006) claim that President John F. Kennedy described the programme as 'the fifty-first state'.

The public inquisitor in action

We will now look at an example of the public inquisitor engaged in their professional practice. A number of analysts have observed that this type of political interview is rather a curious form of interaction. Donald Matheson (2005: 122) goes so far as to describe a celebrated and award winning interview of Jeremy Paxman's as a 'break down' in the rules of conversation and of broadcast interviewing. This was an interview in which Paxman repeats an approximation of the question, 'Did you threaten to overrule him?' 12 times in succession without receiving a direct response. Perhaps, though, instead of looking to the normal rules of conversation, it is more productive to understand these interviews in the context of the overarching discourse of public accountability, in parallel with the conventions of what may be called interview rhetoric. In the case of the Paxman exchange, for example, while the result would be monotonous were it not so comic, the interviewer's strategy might be seen as essentially constructive and informative in emphasizing the wilful failure of the interviewee to answer a question of public concern.

Overall, the terms of engagement in which the public are represented here give rise to often strange communicative situations, the qualities of which become apparent shortly. The extract we will look at now is from the edition of the above-mentioned programme *Meet the Press* broadcast on 26 February 2006 in which Tim Russert interviews governor of California Arnold Schwarzenegger. What emerges is that while the position of Russert as public inquisitor is established by the discursive arrangement of the interview, what often unfolds is a battle between the interviewer and interviewee over ownership of the public voice. Although it should be acknowledged that Schwarzenegger has for some time been a public personality in his own right, and had a long film career before becoming the latest in a line of 'celebrity politicians' to run for public office in the US and elsewhere (Drake and Higgins 2006), the interview has been selected because it is a relatively routine one for *Meet the Press* and for Russert:

TR: Let me take a few minutes and talk about some of the   1
        issues the congressman and the senator were talking
        about. Ports. Do you believe that this deal should go
        forward to allow the United Arab Emirates company
        control six American ports, operate them?   5
AS: Well, first of all, Tim, let me just say that California is
        not affected by that, which is good. Second of all, I think
        that the wise thing was, that the Bush administration
        made and Secretary Chertoff made, was to postpone
        the decision-making and to say, 'Oh, let's give it some   10
        extra time.' Because I think when you see complaints
        coming in like this, you got to study it further, and I
        think that's what they're doing right now. And it's a
        very complex issue, because, you know, we have the
        globalization, we want to do trades with everyone   15
        all over the world, but at the same time, globalization
        crosses with terrorism now, and there's that whole fear.
        And then we have villainized the Arab world also so
        much that now Arab country – or company taking over
        our ports and maybe have some influence in our security,   20
        it freaks everyone out, and rightfully so. So I think you
        have to be really careful. The whole thing as the two
        gentlemen have just discussed is we have to think it
        through and make sure that because – and in the end,
        the number one responsibility of government is to protect   25
        the people of California and the United States.
        This is really the responsibility. That is what you have
        to watch out for. And if we can accomplish that,
        then this company should be able to manage these ports.
        I mean, we have in California, Chinese managing our   30
        ports and have facilities that are leased. We have other
        countries like Japan and South Korea and Denmark and
        so on occupying space. So I think that the trick is just
        how do you do it and protect the people and protect
        our ports.   35
TR: But in principle, you don't have opposition?
AS: I don't have opposition, but it has to be really thought
        through by experts. I'm not an expert in this issue, but
        it has to be thought through by experts, and we
        cannot compromise our security because that would be   40
        terrible if that happens.
TR: You mentioned about Los Angeles. And it is interesting
        because 13 or 14 container terminal operators at the

Los Angeles Long Beach Port are foreign-owned:
China, Japan, Taiwan, Singapore and Denmark, as you   45
said. Are you concerned that China operates a port?
In terms of security?
AS: Well, we have the ultimate control over security. I
mean, they occupy space. They lease space. They
don't own it. And we have Long Beach, for instance,   50
controlling the Long Beach, the ports there. We
have the Coast Guard, we have the customs service,
we have the local law enforcement, we have the Port
Authority. We have all of those agencies, various
different agencies that control it. It's not the Chinese   55
or any other country that control our security. So
I feel very confident with that. And I also feel very
confident with the kind of relationship that we have
with the national Homeland Security Office with
Secretary Chertoff. They have always responded really   60
well to every single one of our concerns that we had.
TR: Let me ask about Iraq because it affects California in
a very big way. These are the numbers of Californians
lost in the war: killed, 242; wounded, 1,857. You now
have 20,000 Californians serving in Iraq, 4,000 of them,   65
National Guard and reserves. Are you concerned that the
National Guard in your state is being depleted by the war?
AS: Sure, it has an effect. And let me tell you something. It
really – it kills me every time when I hear that one of
our officers or someone from the military or National   70
Guard dies over there. It is terrible. And, you know, I
got this morning, for instance, terrible news that
Gregory John Bailey, one of our CHPs, died last night –
yesterday because he was run over by a drunk driver
and while he was ticketing another driver. And when   75
you hear news like that, it is terrible. And, of course,
in this case, my thoughts and prayers go out to his family
and to his friends. You know, it's always – those are
the terrible moments when you're – when you're
governor. When you get this kind of information,   80
you put the flag at half-mast, and you go to some of
the funerals and so on.   82

Meet the Press 1996

Even from this relatively short extract of a far lengthier interview, it
is clear how Russert asserts his responsibility to the political public, in a

manner that involves recourse to classic interviewing techniques. Russert begins by positioning himself within current political concerns by putting to Schwarzenegger an issue highlighted by politicians from an earlier discussion. Tellingly, Schwarzenegger begins by referring to the pertinence of the issue for his own Californian electorate – 'let me say that California is not affected by that, which is good' (lines 6–7) – before returning to that electorate and the US in general later in the same response (line 26). However, Russert does not at this point try to wrest the advocacy of the electorate from Schwarzenegger, but instead steps into the realm of expertise that is demanded of the public inquisitor, where on line 43, Russert brings in specialist information – the number of ports in one of the cities for which Schwarzenegger is responsible that happen to be foreign owned – and calls upon the Governor to account for his position in those terms.

There is, however, one important point at which Russert makes specific reference to the interests of the public, drawing upon Schwarzenegger's own reference to his Californian electorate in order to facilitate a change in topic. Besides the issue of expertise, another quality of this form of public advocacy is the capacity to ask questions on a range of subjects, with no need to explain these transitions by any terms other than the broad issue of public concern. The somewhat abrupt change of topic takes place on line 62, where Russert shifts from ownership of US ports onto the war in Iraq. Although a duty of care to the public has already been cited by Schwarzenegger, the question from Russert 'Let me ask about Iraq, because it affects Californians in a very big way' puts this relationship between the interview and public concern in more explicit terms, asserting both the governor's responsibility to his electorate and Russert's duty to ask questions on their behalf. It is at this point that the qualities of public representation and expertise combine, where Russert follows his claim to speak as a consequence of the interests of Californians by substantiating their concern with a list of the numbers of state casualties. What's more, the modality of Russert's phrasing – 'these are the numbers' (line 63) – implies, perhaps without justification, that this information may have been new to Schwarzenegger as well as to the public at large. Explicit references to a concern for the political public are therefore important enough to be fought over, and the institutional positioning of the interviewer as operating in the public interest is crucial to understanding the terms of such exchanges.

These other factors besides the content of the interview itself amount to what Austin (1962) calls 'the felicity conditions' – that is, 'the criteria [for] a speech act to serve its purpose' (Crystal 1997: 150) – and these allow the accomplishment of an authoritative form of journalistic discourse (Raymond 2000). In the UK at least, the activities of these 'public inquisitors' extend beyond the formal political interview to include similar forms of questioning in other media genres (Higgins 2008). A variety of media formats provide a vehicle for the discursive figure of the public inquisitor to be realized in other contexts, including the intellectual quiz show, and the writing of books advocating positions on such politically charged issues as the hidden layers of the ruling elite (in the case of Jeremy Paxman) and falling food standards (in the case of John Humphrys). In the same way, one of the elements that substantiate the authority of such inquisitors as NBC's Tim Russert is the extent to which he has become a celebrity journalist. Russert has developed a personal standing that has a direct bearing on his capacity to stand up to well-known political figures. In the case of Paxman and Humphrys of the BBC, their credentials as public advocates may be argued to have reached a wider public through their activities outside of the formal political realm, such that those activities help substantiate their fame either as questioners or as politically concerned citizens themselves. A similar example of this engagement of the public advocate as wider media figure occurred when Tim Russert appeared as himself on cop show *Homicide: Life on the Streets*. Russert is also a public personality in a number of other ways. He has written a book on his relationship with his father and won such non-professional accolades as the National Fatherhood Initiative 'Father of the year' and *Parents* magazine 'Dream dad' (*Meet the Press* 2006). Importantly, that public persona to emerge needs to remain in keeping with those performances of duty and integrity associated with the role of the public inquisitor.

However this extends beyond the media persona of the journalist – which depends, after all, on the prior knowledge of the viewer – such that this form of representing the political public also comes armed with a number of visual codes. These codes are primarily embodied, what Robert Hodge and Gunther Kress (1988: 61) refer to as 'ideologies of ways of sitting', beginning the introduction with a head and shoulder shot of the journalist, the direct address to camera, business wear, and ties in the case of male presenters. Of course, it should be acknowledged that even the most long-standing of these codes is subject to a gradual change in accordance with the wider social environment. The early management of BBC radio, in particular, was notable for requiring announcers to dress in formal evening wear, with what would now be considered a businesslike ensemble then dismissed as a mere 'lounge suit'. As part of a broader deformalization of news presentation, Kress and van Leeuwen (2001) place performance at the centre of the discourse. In a discussion of how performances intervene in and 'animate' the mean-ings of such discursive elements as design and script, they suggest the driving force of this semiotic environment is the 'active signifying' of interviewing such as Russert's (Kress and van Leeuwen 2001: 86). The mode of performance associated with the public inquisitor is intended as one of severity of purpose and professionalism, but the role also begets the construction – at least in rhetorical terms – of a new form of public, with specifically political concerns and a sharply cynical edge.

Political coverage and populism

While we have so far chosen to dwell on the positioning and the mediated persona of the public inquisitor, an important component of this form of public representation has been the appeal to the people, a strategy that is characteristic of a form of populism (Clayman 2002: 211–12). There are a number of strands to the use of populism, and while it is often used to describe political movements based around ideas of a 'popular will' normally embodied in the 'charismatic leader' (Kazin 1995) our intention here is to explore its use as a form of political rhetoric. Across both interpretations, Koen Abts and Stefan Rummens (2007: 409) emphasize the importance of Margaret Canovan's (2002) observation that populism functions as a strategy rather than a political ideal – offering a 'thin-centred ideology' to be filled out by any of an infinite variety of political discourses. In practices of rhetoric, however, the function of appeals to 'the people' are clearer, offering 'a central signifier which receives a fundamentally monolithic interpretation' (Abts and Rummens 2007: 408). Populist rhetoric of whatever hue, according to Abts and Rummens, simply sets up popular interest as a 'redemptive force' against the 'shortcomings and broken promises' of the expert, representative system.

For all this, the relationship between populism and the political interviewer is a complex one. We could certainly look over the practices of the public inquisitor and detect a significant element of populist hostility to an elite system that is implicitly given as inherently untrustworthy and corrupt. On the other hand, critics such as David Croteau and William Hoynes (1994) have suggested that such interview arrangements are a device for members of the system to speak between themselves in a manner that merely offers an empty performance of political engagement. In this section we will look at a form of populist engagement that deliberately eschews much of the performed exception-alness and expertise that forms part of the inquisitional practices described above.

In one of a pair of classic studies of a UK news and magazine programme of the 1970s and early 1980s called *Nationwide*, Charlotte Brunsdon and David Morley describe what they call a 'populist ventriloquism', where the voice of the ordinary public appears to find form in the voice of one well-known individual. This is not the intellectual voice speaking on behalf of the public that we encounter in the informed and demonstrably well educated Tim Russert or Robin Day. Instead, this is a voice that comes from the ordinary people and shares their diction and vocabulary. This means, according to Brunsdon and Morley (1978: 7), that 'the discourse of *Nationwide* is designed to be relatively closed; [noting that] the stress on 'making the issues comprehensible', translating them into 'real terms' leaves little space for interpretation'. They describe what this might mean for party politics:

> Implicit in this perspective is a populist ideology that takes for granted the irrelevance of 'politics' to the real business of everyday life ('Whichever party is in power I'll still not have a job. Prices will still rise ...') and also takes for granted the disillusionment of the electorate with 'politicians' and their promises
>
> (Brunsdon and Morley 1978: 7)

What populist ventriloquism seeks to do, then, is to disengage the public from politics, and filter public access to politics through a particular form of discourse. At root, this form of populism asserts that meaningful discussion concerns events and consequences rather than policies and arguments. The possibilities this allows for misrepresenting the individual case or unforeseen catastrophe as indicators of broader political failings is clear. A discussion that begins and ends with the individual sees every untended patient as the death knell of Medicare or the National Health Service and every errant migrant or refugee as reason to impose tighter border restrictions. Perhaps most importantly, the form of political discussion that this engenders makes it all the more difficult to provide insight into longer term policy direction.

It may be, as Jeffrey Scheuer (2001: 123) suggests, that a simplifying form of rhetoric has dire implications for political culture, but many major news networks believe that it offers a compelling option. While it stemmed from a specific controversy rather than a change in the long term strategy in the station's coverage of political issues, the replacement of Dan Rather in 2006 as chief news presenter of CBS offers an insight into the tension between the forms of public advocacy we have outlined. Dan Rather fits the description of the public advocate described above, and has been regularly accused of undue aggression in interviews (Schudson 1995: 92). He has also stood against what he sees as the 'showbizification' of news broadcasting (Schudson 1995: 6). Dan

Rather's departure from his prominent position at CBS was hastened by his involvement in a story concerning President George W. Bush that was shown to have been based upon unsubstantiated documents, and he was immediately replaced by long-standing correspondent Bob Schieffer. While the appointment of Schieffer was a temporary one, it nonetheless marked a significant moment in which CBS opted for a more 'folksy' style of news (Stanley 2006). The inclination of this more personable form of advocacy is to emphasize and engage with a reading of the likely emotive reaction of the audience, far more than offering a demonstrable concern to bring expertise to bear. In keeping with this style, Schieffer's on-air response to the foreign owned ports story discussed at length by Tim Russert and Governor Schwarzenegger was, for example, the mock bamboozlement of 'this is fairly weird; there is no other way to put it' (Stanley 2006).

Yet, while there are populist or 'folksy' elements to much of the coverage of politics, it is important to stress that there is not a straightforward opposition between this and the role of public advocacy. To illustrate, here is an extract from a 2004 interview between Australia's Channel 9 presenter Laurie Oakes and Australian prime minister John Howard.

LO:	So were you up all night bleary eyed watching the Olympics?	1
JH:	Quite a bit of it. And some football to boot as well.	
LO:	It's a pretty good start for Australia.	
JH:	A very good start. I think the Australian public are enjoying the Olympics.	5
LO:	Meaning you won't interrupt them?	
JH:	Well, I think they're enjoying it. And I'm – I'm enjoying them and I think the opening was a great triumph for Greece. They've had a lot of bad luck with a couple of their stars. We feel a particular affinity for the Greeks, because so many Australians came from there, and I think the Games have got off to a wonderful start, and I think there'll be a lot of focus on them now – I'm part of that focus. Not totally. I've got other things I've got in my mind as well, but I think the public is pretty keen on following the Games at present.	10 15
LO:	So I think we can take from that we don't need to worry about an election imminently. But what did you think of Ian Thorpe's swim and the women freestyle relay team?	20
JH:	Well, I was particularly impressed with the freestyle. Because it's a while since we have won that. And I think	

	there was perhaps a greater expectation in relation to	
	Thorpe and Hackett, but expectations bring with them	
	additional pressures.	25
LO:	Now, even though you're not going to interrupt the	
	Olympics with a campaign, I'd like to ask you about the	
	kind of election we can expect. Mark Latham wants	
	three leader debates.	
JH:	Mm.	30
LO:	Will you go along with that?	
JH:	Oh, no, I think what we'll have is one debate. Which	
	we've had in the past. The first time I was opposition	
	leader I didn't even get one. In 1987 Bob Hawke refused	
	to debate me at all. In the last two elections we've had a	35
	debate, and as far as I'm concerned there should be a	
	debate. I'm perfectly happy to have a debate. When	
	the election is called then we'll have some – we'll have	
	the usual discussions about the format of that. But I'm	
	perfectly happy to debate him, but one debate's	40
	appropriate in my view.	41

(Media Monitors 2004)

It is clear from the context that John Howard has been called in for a political interview, but Oakes begins by asking a number of questions on Australia's performance at the Olympic Games. Importantly, these are not questions that intend to hold Howard accountable for Australian fortunes – although they might well have been put that way – but are instead presented as friendly chat, with informal phrasing such as 'bleary eyed' and 'pretty good start', and inviting personal responses from Howard. It turns out, however, that the convivial sports talk is a strategy for Oakes to disorientate his interviewee before getting around to introducing the issue of whether Howard has imminent plans to call an election. To put this in terms of rhetorical technique, Oakes heads off any strategies of question avoidance that Howard might use by necessitating a shift in what Goffman (1981) terms his conversational 'footing', from the relaxed poise of someone involved in open sports chatter to one engaged as a subject of political questioning. What emerges is a combination of informal chat with public advocacy, which is sustained even until line 19 when a political inference is place alongside another sports question, and not conceded until line 26 when Oates acknowledges the prime minister's hints that the election will, after all, come after the Olympics.

There are also visual elements to what we can call this popularization of public advocacy. Although Kress and van Leeuwen (2001) emphasize their relative contingency, even when mixing sports chat with political analysis and offering folksy 'gee whiz' comments to developing stories, traditional signs of the bardic function of news, such as the business suit and the direct address to camera, remain intact for now. The iconic desk, on the other hand, has become a candidate for sacrifice. While the desk's removal is not common across political and news programming, many presenters now deliver the news standing in front of the camera. The majority of newscasters in the UK now punctuate the news stories by sweeping around the studio in what is a 'kinetic' performance of productive movement (Corner 2003: 69). British parliamentarian and media critic Chris Mullin (2006) dismisses this as 'emoting' to camera rather than sticking to the task of appraising the public of the facts. In the case of the most prominent newscasters, moreover, this mode of performance is presented alongside their roles as an interviewer of major politicians and policy makers. While the visual and rhetorical practices that give the public inquisitor 'credibility' are often those signs that connote authority across the wider cultural and institutional environment, Kress and van Leeuwen (2001: 111) argue that this dominant discursive regime is continually beholden to innovative discursive practices. It follows that these systems of sign will develop within broadcasting as surely as they change outside.

Alternative advocacy: the entertainment talk show

In our discussion of public advocacy in media, we have considered the introduction of popular elements to these forms of engagement with the political public. As shown in Leo Braudy's (1997) history of fame, a relationship between politics and popular culture is certainly not a novel combination. However, recent decades have seen this association become a matter of debate (Street 2001). In the last decade particularly, an increasing number of politicians have chosen to forego the style of interview associated with the public inquisitor in favour of the entertainment talk show. In the coverage of politics in France, the generic type that Neveu (2005) calls 'sofa programmes' have assumed prominence over established formats. Also, former UK prime minister Tony Blair supplemented his appearances on political talk shows such as *Newsnight, NBC Nightly News*, and *Breakfast with Frost* with entertainment talk shows such as *This Morning, The Frank Skinner Show* and *Richard and Judy*. When Arnold Schwarzenegger announced his intention to run for the governorship of California, furthermore, he chose to do so as a guest on the entertainment programme *The Tonight Show with Jay Leno* (Drake and Higgins 2006: 95).

Taking the 2000 US presidential election as his focus, Matthew Baum (2005) reflects upon why appearances on talk shows have become such a prominent feature of the modern political campaign. This crossover of formats, Baum notes, runs contrary to the argument that the public are disengaged from politics, such that the appearance of politicians tends to produce larger rather than smaller audiences (Baum 2005: 214). While, at least in part, this might result from a desire on the audience's part to see politicians squirm within an unfamiliar format, Baum argues that talk shows do also appear to be effective in enabling politicians to win over a significant sector of the electorate. In particular, politically disengaged citizens who nonetheless had the intention of voting for one candidate are more likely to claim to have been won over to the other side as a result of entertainment talk shows (Baum 2005: 217). The shows therefore appear to be effective in tapping into what are generally known as 'floating' voters, and specifically appearances give access to those not inspired to watch conventional political programmes such as *Meet the Press* (Baum 2005: 214). To place Baum's argument within the broader history of the study of political communications, entertainment talk shows are invested with a level of trust on the part of the viewer that Katz and Lazarsfeld (1964) would associate with the role of those 'opinion leaders' empowered to gather political information and pass it on in an easily comprehensible form.

It may be said that the political fortunes to emerge from the talk show circuit seem to depend upon a particular form of political impression management, which relies more upon the image of the candidate than the quality of the arguments (Louw 2005: 172). Baum (2005: 214) writes that the topicality of the interviews betrays a primary interest in the personalities of the candidates, particularly when the candidate shows personal qualities or relates anecdotes that might be unexpected or endearingly quirky. So in a similar pattern to that which emerges from Neveu's (2005) discussion of political coverage in France, the emphasis is on allowing the politician to construct themselves as open and personable. This has implications for the forms of disclosure required and the interview techniques used to secure this, which contrast markedly with formal political programmes such as *Meet the Press* and *Face the Nation*. Baum (2005: 222) found that whereas four out of five statements on interviewees within formal political programmes could be designated as critical, similar statements and interjections on entertainment talk shows over the course of the same campaign were overwhelmingly positive. The form of discourse that the entertainment talk show represents therefore appears to stand in stark contrast to the interrogative mode of the public advocate. Even when questions are considered relatively tough by talk show standards – a David Letterman interview with George W. Bush was considered so 'hardball' as to be newsworthy on that basis – the most pointed of Letterman's questions was not deemed hostile by Baum (2005: 230). In discharging their duty for public disclosure in this way, politicians themselves are therefore free to concentrate on 'tailoring political messages to the [entertainment] talk show audiences', which means focusing on their personality rather than their beliefs and policies (2005: 230).

Yet, as our discussion of the ways media represent the public has shown, the use of 'personality' towards political ends cuts both ways, and strategies of persona and creditability are as open to the talk show host as they are to the interviewer. While a number of hosts, such as David Letterman, express misgivings over the legitimacy of political arguments that may be derived from a form of engagement geared towards the generation of laughter rather than ideology (Jones 2005: 55), Jeffrey Jones discusses the representative potential of these hosts as 'public proxies'. Jones's description of the comedian talk show host seems to offer a mix of what Higgins (2008) calls as the public inquisitor, on the one hand, and what Brunsdon and Morley (1978) describe as the popular ventriloquist, on the other. They craft 'personas built on paradoxes: smart and savvy yet an everyman; speaking common sense through a common vernacular about politics, yet retaining uncommon knowledge of trivial or arcane cultural references, being both a cynic and an idealist, a postmodern yet thoroughly modern man' (Jones 2005: 122). In this chapter, we have examined a non-comedic example of this. In his interview with the Australian prime minister, Laurie Oates demonstrates the rhetorical strategies that are opened to those interviewers choosing to mix political discussion with broader cultural references, in a manner designed to wrong-foot an interviewee seeking to withhold political information. While the implicit gendered quality of his summary of public representation is clear, Jones suggests it is their 'popular' qualities that lend talk show hosts their political effectiveness.

Conclusion

Drawing upon the distinctions we have just outlined between the various forms of public advocacy, a number of interesting issues arise from a reading of John Hartley's (1992) work on universal versus adversarial journalism. For Hartley, universal and adversarial forms of journalism draw upon two distinct configurations of 'truth'. Universal forms of knowledge and truth telling, for which he names such champions as John Milton and Samuel Johnson, presents what Hartley calls an unsullied 'virginal truth' before an audience that in principle ought to include the entire human race (Hartley 1992: 165). Adversarial truth, on the other hand, was born out of such conflicts as the American and French revolutions, where certain versions of truth began to usurp and dominate others – truth had become relative and subject to argument. Hartley (1992: 169) describes this shift as engendering a transformation in a form of audience from the common reader to a particular, targeted readership. Notably, Hartley argues, those fond of the idea of universal truth and who address themselves to the world at large have tended also to oppose social change and development, Winston Churchill for example. Whereas those others, such as Thomas Paine, who argue instead that truth is a matter of adversarialism and argument tend to be of a radical stripe. We have discussed the merits of adversarial journalism at some length, and perhaps see echoes of the opposite 'universal' approach to truth in Brunsdon and Morley's (1978) description of the 'closed discourse' we see in populism. On this basis at least, there seems to be an argument for saying that while populist ventriloquism pretends to plain speaking, its denial of the nuances of truth and argument may inherently favour the forces of conservatism.

Yet in this chapter we have seen emerge a more optimistic assessment of the possibilities of public representation in media, particularly in how it has developed alongside forms of popular culture. It will be especially useful to reflect further upon politically motivated entertainment television, such as *Politically Incorrect* in the US and *Bremner, Bird and Fortune* in the UK in engaging a developing form of political public. In a critical discussion of conventional political broadcasting, Jones (2005: 36) argues that a significant sector of the politically active public see programmes such as *Meet the Press* as little more than knowing rituals between members of a self-serving political elite. This has echoes of Croteau and Hoynes's (1994) position that so-called hardball interviews involve more knowing spectacle than substance. In this chapter, we have also seen how the development of forms of personality-based journalism in such programmes, aligned with the joining of political and popular forms, both address a politically engaged public and empower its representatives in developing and interesting ways.

Questions for discussion

- What are the limitations and dangers of a communicative environment in which media embody the public interest, in the context of either:
  i) a state subsidized media arrangement?

ii) a market driven media system?

- Does the cultivation on their part of a 'media persona' help or impede the work of a journalist in how they represent the public?

Further reading

Clayman, S. and Heritage, J. (2002) *The News Interview*. Cambridge: Cambridge University Press.

Talbot, M. (2007) *Media Discourse: Representation and Interaction*. Edinburgh: Edinburgh University Press.

4   The political public take to the stage

Introduction

At the beginning of the last chapter we noted that there were two main ways of representing the political public in media. In that chapter we explored the first of these, which involved media institutions acting on behalf of the public in what we described as an advocacy model. In this chapter, we will now turn to the second direction in which the political public is represented in media, where our concentration will be on those genres of political media constructed around notions of public participation. We will look at a number of the different ways in which the public are integrated into particular media genres, developing those arguments around 'the public sphere' developed in Chapter 2 to discuss the manner in which political debates are facilitated and engaged. Throughout the chapter, we will be concerned with examining the terms of these political debates according to the discursive restrictions of the formats, as well as with how much these forms of public participation in the political media truly enables the free circulation of arguments.

Public participation: motives and types

According to Brian McNair et al. (2003), politically based public participation programming offers three main advantages for broadening political engagement. First of all, such programmes present a means by which the public can have first-hand 'representation' in mass media in a tangible manifestation of a mediated public sphere (McNair et al. 2003: 31). Across television and radio – and latterly through the Internet – members of the public can enter the media apparatus to listen to their peers and offer political arguments on the basis of a shared concern in the democratic process. The second advantage stems from the opportunities of public access to those in political influence, where members of the public have the chance to submit policy makers and members of the political elite to scrutiny and questioning (McNair et al. 2003: 57). A third advantage of this form of programming is that it might prompt what McNair et al. call the 'mobilization' of the political public; the possibility, that is to say, that viewers and participants be impelled to 'act on, or at least think about, the issues under discussion' (McNair et al. 2003: 64). Thus, at the level at which media make a normative assessment of their own contribution to public service, giving the public a participatory role in political television both actualizes the mediated public sphere as described in Chapter 2, and potentially contributes to solving the problem of public disengagement from formal politics.

As to the terms of this drive towards public inclusion, McNair et al. (2003: 33) describe this as 'public access broadcasting' and highlight three main forms. One is the occasional 'single issue debate', where a studio audience is assembled to debate an issue of particular interest or importance – sometimes as a follow-up to a controversial current affairs programme or documentary. The other two types are regularly scheduled programming genres. One of these is the 'studio debate', which is relatively unusual but important in political programming, in which a representative audience is invited to ask questions of an assemblage of 'politicians and/or suitably qualified experts' (McNair et al. 2003: 33), and we will go on to look at an example of this later. The second and most common of these genres is the 'phone-in debate', which normally takes place on radio and where listeners are invited to call in to make points or ask questions.

McNair et al. confine their definition of the phone-in debate, or 'talk radio' to those programmes in which politicians or specialists are placed at the callers' disposal. As we will see, however, a significant tradition of talk radio has developed in which the conversation is contained between the host and the caller, and in which the topic is subject to continual shift at the behest of the host and production team, sometimes on the basis of a caller intervention. These practices are particularly character-istic of scheduled talk shows based around the branded personality of the host – such as Rush Limbaugh in the US – as well as of dedicated talk stations, such as BBC Radio 5 in the UK (Starkey 2004). In order to fully explore this capacity of radio to participate in the expression of a political public, our discussion in this chapter will extend consideration of the construction of the political public in media through modes of participation across both television and radio.

The political public as studio audience

One option for public participation is through the use of a studio audience. It is often the case that a studio audience is used to represent a broadcast's wider public. In large part, the studio audience is an aide towards what Paddy Scannell (1996) calls 'broadcast sociability', which in this case describes the enactment of a dynamic social relationship with the watching or listening audience that is designed to address them as individuals rather than as an ill defined mass (see Scannell 1991: 3). It is conventional for situation comedies, for example, to be filmed in front of a studio audience in order to generate a live response that is often wrongly assumed to be recorded, 'canned' laughter: providing the input of what Carpignano et al. (1990) call an 'audible public'. In that case, the reaction of the studio audience provides a form of punctuation for significant moments in the performance, such as the entrance of a main character or the delivery of a punch line. What the presence of the studio audience serves to do is to signal the appropriateness of emotional reactions, with a view to generating relatively similar responses in the broadcast audience. Thus, the working rationale is that the studio audience will provide an enthusiastic version of the audience watching at home. We will see that a similar mode of representation is introduced when the political public are admitted to the studio, albeit that the purposes for their being there are presented as far more onerous and the terms of their participation are certainly more complex.

While we will be looking again at audience participation television in Chapter 6 and will be discussing how much they engage with matters of broad public concern, for now we will be looking at a number of discussion programmes that concentrate solely on matters of current political policy. Another subtle but important difference in these political programmes is that whereas the great majority of audience participation television productions are filmed in a central studio – indeed, in the case of the *Jerry Springer Show*, travelling to the location of the studio became one of the selling points – the programmes we examine in this chapter move around different population centres across the country, in what could be loosely called a roadshow format. The programmes we look at are produced in the UK; *Question Time* and *Any Questions?* by BBC Television and BBC Radio, and *Jonathan Dimbleby* by ITV. The programmes are widely seen as closely related – not least because *Any Questions* and *Jonathan Dimbleby* are both presented and chaired by Jonathan Dimbleby, while his brother David Dimbleby chairs *Question Time* – and all are considered flagship programmes in UK political broadcasting. The overall rhetoric that surrounds these productions is that they provide a site for the rehearsal of political debates between citizens, and that they bring politicians and policy makers to account for their conduct before a selection of interested members of the political public.

The arrangement of the discussants on these programmes is significant. In terms of how they are defined and how their contributions to the programme are managed, the participants are divided into two groups: a number of panel members – usually limited to around four – and a much larger studio audience. *Jonathan Dimbleby* provides an exception to this, by only having one interviewee to take questions. The proceedings are adjudicated by the programme presenter, who holds the position of chair and selects questioners from the audience to put points to the panel. The panel are usually chosen to represent the conventional range of the political establishment, from the conservative wing, liberal wing, and centre of parliamentary politics. The fourth panel member usually comes from a non-governmental political organization or special interest group, although McNair (2000: 113) notes a tendency in recent years to select the fourth panel member from a fairly broad spectrum of public life, often including musicians and comedians, for example. It is important to note that any ordinance on the programme's part to represent a wider range of political views is not altogether self-imposed, and is at least in part to be seen to meet the UK public service obligations set out in Chapter 1 to be politically even-handed. Certainly, the composition of the panel ensures that the governing party of the day is always outnumbered (Starkey 2007: 135).

In order to fully understand the dynamics of these programmes, it is important to see them as debates, or competitions between sets of already established political views and positions of interest. Ian Hutchby (2006) offers an analysis of an edition of *Question Time* from the perspective of 'conversation analysis'. Conversation analysis is interested in the dynamics of interaction and language as it is used in order to discern the patterns that emerge from given contexts. Hutchby looks at the production of 'political alignments' in the debate on *Question Time*, and finds that the successful alignments are recognizable within the debate itself, as opposed to purely on the basis of such extra-discursive factors as the political histories of the personalities themselves. Since the political affiliations of the participants are outlined at the outset of the programme in any event, this suggests an overall discursive environment in which allegiances in the political field figure prominently.

In addition, conversational techniques are often geared towards generating a positive response in the studio audience, utilizing such forms of political rhetoric as the 'claptrap'; this being the crescendo of a pleasing of passage of speech, designed principally for the response it is likely to generate (Atkinson 1984: 47). Hutchby (2006: 143) looks at UK member of parliament Michael Heseltine's use of a popular form of claptrap, where he transforms his position at the beginning of the sequence as the object of audience derision to one in which he produces a 'three part list' of items to whip up audience approval. We should note how much is therefore integrated into the performance of the politicians themselves, in terms of both their embodied displays and their capacity to switch in and out of explicitly inclusive forms of rhetoric. Our immediate interest is less focused on the flourishes of political rhetoric that can be used to generate audience applause, however, and is more concerned with the routine way in which the studio audience is manifest a political force, and the controls that are placed on this function.

Laurie Anderson (1999) provides an analysis of political public participation programmes that, first of all, sees them as 'embedded contexts', with internal rules of conduct, decorum and appropriateness of expression, and therefore as peculiar sorts of public stage for the 'performance' of representation. Appropriately geared performances often bring forth collective forms of audience response, such as laughter, choruses of disapproval and applause (Anderson 1999: 77). However, in a discussion of ITV's *Jonathan Dimbleby*, one of the things that Anderson finds is most significant about these programmes is how much individual audience members work at being representative of absent others, by stressing their 'group membership' credentials. When first called upon to offer a contribution, Anderson (1999: 57) finds that audience members tend to stress their national identity, political affiliation or their professional/occupational experience. These, he argues, operate as a 'warrant ... to authorise the speaker to intervene as a spokesperson for the group in question' (Anderson 1999: 58). These practices of representativeness are also emphasized by the chair of the programme, who will routinely announce an audience member designated to speak by specifying their professional group or occupation, a practice also followed by BBC's *Question Time*. Indeed, when unexpected points are raised by the panel, the chair does on occasion ask whether a person suitably representative of a particular group is to be found in that week's audience (Anderson 1999: 62). It is important to note, however, that this process of labelling is informed by the political underpinnings of the programme, which in all three cases can be loosely defined as the defence of UK democracy – and Anderson (1999: 69) points out an example in which an audience member presenting themselves as one of 'the Irish people' is redefined from the chair as a member of a more restricted group when it emerges that their point is in favour of the Irish nationalist group Sinn Fein. That is, their voice was not deemed to be admissible as a member of the UK public but of an outside grouping. In contrast, those speaking against Sinn Fein were permitted to proceed on the basis of a much wider form of representation. In other words, an agreed set of responsibilities that limits the legitimacy of speaking on behalf of the political public is integral to the conduct of the programme.

This extract of BBC Radio 4's *Any Questions?* is taken from the programme broadcast on 20 January 2006, and offers a number of insights into how this benign system of control is maintained over the audience and the panel. *Any Questions?* offers a complex arrangement of turn-taking and supplementary questions, and the extract is necessarily lengthy. The panel for that week comprises two members of the UK House of Lords, Charlie Falconer (CF) and Shirley Williams (SW), representing the UK Labour party and Liberal Democrats respectively, with the right-of-centre Conservative party and government opposition represented by the member of parliament Theresa Villiers (TV). The fourth place is taken by George Pascoe-Watson (GPW), who had recently become editor of the UK's highest selling popular tabloid newspaper the *Sun*. In keeping with the requirement to place a selection of political voices before the public, and to be seen to allow all the participants to give their own answers to any questions, the chair Jonathan Dimbleby (JD) signals the member of the audience to put the initial question, the identity of whom is decided by the production team in advance, and then selects each of the responding panel members by name.

JD:	Our first question please.	1
Aud:	Jill Hoganchor. Will the outcome of the Iraq election perpetuate sectarian violence?	
JD:	Shirley Williams.	
SW:	I have to say that I was quite relieved that the Shia,	5
	although they got by far the largest single vote, didn't	
	actually get an overall majority and therefore will have	
	to form a coalition because I think the Shia who have	
	come to power having been out of it for a very long	
	time, they were clearly heavily discriminated against	10
	by Saddam Hussein when he was dictator of Iraq, have	
	got to in a sense learn for themselves the compromise	
	and the understandings and the tolerance that are part	
	of being part of a democratic society. And I think the	
	fact they will have to work with either the Kurds or the	15
	Sunnis, almost certainly at the moment with the Kurds,	
	may be helpful because the great danger for Iraq is	
	being blown apart, is being imploded into three	
	separate parts which represent each of the peoples of	
	Iraq. And this now means I think there's a real chance,	20
	not a very good chance but still a chance, that Iraq	
	may remain united, may hold together and may slowly	
	develop a government that can represent the whole	
	country but it's not going to be easy going.	
JD:	And not a coalition of Shiites and Kurds against, as it	25

	were, the Sunnis because the Kurds have no affection	
	for the Sunnis either?	
SW:	Of course that's the danger but an even greater danger	
	would have been the Shia gets everybody else.	
JD:	Thank you. Theresa Villiers.	30
TV:	I mean I certainly sort of find it heart warming	
	that the democratic process is getting started in Iraq.	
	I think the Iraqi people are going to need a huge	
	amount of support in taking that process forward. I mean	
	we've got to bear in mind that it took us in this country	35
	literally hundreds of years to build a functioning	
	democracy, it is very, very difficult to build a democracy	
	in a matter of months. But I would welcome a coalition	
	between two of the groups or even a government of	
	national unity to design, to build confidence and to	40
	draw the three communities together to build trust	
	between the three communities and hopefully really to	
	find – to isolate the insurgents and give Iraq a real	
	democratic and peaceful future.	
JD:	Lord Falconer.	45
CF:	I don't know precisely what the future will hold. There's	
	been lots of gloomy prognostications about Iraq	
	but they successfully elected an assembly to decide	
	on a constitution. Again despite grim prognostications	
	that assembly did agree a constitution, it was then	50
	approved in a referendum and again tonight we've just	
	heard on the news, just before we started, that there	
	have been successful elections to what is the	
	equivalent of a parliament. Now I don't know how it	
	will end but I am quite sure the Iraqi people want for	55
	themselves what we want for them – freedom, democracy	
	and the ability to go about their business in peace. And	
	this is the best hope for them. And if it works it will	
	deliver not just for Iraq but for the whole of the region a	
	new future and we should do all that we can to support	60
	them. I don't know whether it'll succeed but I very much	
	hope it will.	
JD:	You may have missed it but in the same bulletin we heard	
	that yet another English individual working for the	
	Americans has been killed. You answered that question as	65
	if they wasn't – hadn't been a huge upsurge in suicide	
	bombings, killing mayhem, kidnappings.	
CF:	I should say every time that there is another	

democratic opportunity in Iraq the insurgency goes up
and nothing I say should be taken to underestimate in   70
any way the security difficulties there. But surely what
we should be aiming for is a political solution and a
political solution is that the differences within a
country, like in our country, are dealt with through
politics and I don't know if they'll get there in Iraq   75
but the steps I've just referred to are the right steps to
be there on their way.

JD: George Pascoe-Watson.

GPW: Yeah and our thoughts obviously go tonight to the
family of the British man killed out in Iraq as they   80
naturally would. And I think your questioner – our
questioner tonight was asking whether or not she
thought that the chances of insurgencies would go up
again and I happen to think that the history has
shown us that every time that there's been an   85
opportunity for democracy there has been a greater
increase in violence. And that's really to be expected –
that nation building in the way that is underway is
not an easy job and it's particularly difficult exercise
given Iraq's history. I've always been prepared for this   90
kind of violence, I've been to Iraq three times since
the war ended and I covered the war itself. And there
is a huge feeling among most Iraqis that they do
want the democratic process. It does mean that
American and British soldiers are going to have to be   95
there for many, many years, perhaps 10 years or more,
which is an unfortunate side of the big decision we
took to go to war. The chances of violence continuing
I'm afraid are there but slowly and surely we're
getting there.   100

JD: Shirley Williams.

SW: Well I wanted to come back because I thought that
Charlie Falconer was being a bit frankly complacent
about it. What worries me is that we now know that as
of the end of this year the United States will not   105
put in any more money for reconstruction, they've
announced that, their $18 billion which they voted
for in 2003 comes to an end in 2006 and no more
money will be voted. Now what worries me is that
neither the electricity output, the gas output, the water 110
systems – none of these domestic infrastructure systems

are back where they were in 19 – in 2002 when the
invasion – just before the invasion occurred and we
now have the information that the reconstruction money
will be shut off. I agree with George that what we want   115
to see – and with Theresa – that what we want to see
is a solid successful democracy in Iraq but I cannot
see how cutting off all the money to reconstruct the
country is going to be a major contribution to that.

JD: Thank you. We'll leave that there and go to our next.   120

(BBC 2006)

The chair's introduction of the panel members to each stage of the
debate is notable in its crispness. In a discussion of phone-in
conversations, Tolson (2006: 35) remarks that in much public participation media there is no obligation to engage in such rituals as the
exchange of greetings or negotiated ending. But these extracts go beyond
even this. In place of such everyday politeness strategies as a direct or
indirect request to speak ('would you now like to answer . . .' or 'perhaps
you would like to answer') Dimbleby simply announces the turn of each
panel member by stating their name. In the same way as the role of the
public inquisitors described in the last chapter, Dimbleby is engaged in a
knowing performance that switches between severity and light heart-
edness.

However, although the ground for this outward abruptness is the
maintenance of the neutrality of the chair, it is also apparent that the
ordering of these introductions is invested with meaning. This
organization is influenced by the questions put by the audience. Often,
questions are directed more to one member of the panel than the others,
usually because of their political affiliation or governmental responsibility. On other occasions, a question will arise that will illicit a more
controversial response from one panel member than the others. The
convention in both cases has become for the chair to call that panel
member either first or last. Often, where panel members are closely
involved in the matter, the chair will opt for last in order to maximize
audience anticipation. In this case, Shirley Williams (SW) is called both
as the initial respondent in line 4 and as the last respondent in line 102.
While both were signalled by the chair in the same way, the context of
the second obliges Williams to respond to the other contributions;
something acknowledged by Williams when she says in line 102 'Well I
wanted to come back because I thought that Charlie Falconer was being
a bit frankly complacent about it'.

As well as engaging in an artful performance of neutrality in ordering
speakers, designed to maximize debate among the panel as well as

anticipation in the audience, Dimbleby offers his own response to two of the four initial answers. In line 25, for example, Dimbleby asks Williams to explore a scenario not considered in her answer, and then in line 63 Dimbleby uses a pretext of updating Falconer on a recent news event to suggest the panellist is understating the level of unrest in Iraq. The chair routinely asks supplementary questions, often asking for elaboration on key points or correcting errors of fact. This practice offers an insight of a further duty of the chair in this programme, which is to decide whether a question has been given an adequate response. In large part, the chair brings into the *Any Questions* studio elements of those forms of embodied public representativeness we discussed in the last chapter.

There is also an equal crispness to the manner in which the audience members are invited to present their question. *Any Questions?* does not engage in the same identification practices as the television programmes *Jonathan Dimbleby* or *Question Time* by giving a name and personal context to each questioner in the first instance (Anderson 1999: 58). Rather, *Any Questions?* simply requests 'our first question please' (line 1). While it may be argued that this denies any specific 'representational warrant' to the audience member by specifying their claim to public representativeness, Anderson (1999: 61) argues that this implicitly extends to that speaker 'the opportunity to portray their opinion as representation of absent others' in a far wider sense. It seems, therefore, there are at least two options for representing the audience participant as a member of the public. They might, on the one hand, be presented as a citizen with particular interests and concerns likely to be shared by others, perhaps members of a similar gender, ethnic or social grouping, or they might be invited to offer an implied expression of public interest as a whole.

But even besides these taxonomies of representation, there are other considerations of direct audience control and definition by the figure of the chair, which can be identified in this routine exchange from the same broadcast.

JD:	Thank you very much. [CLAPPING] After that I'll just ask	1
	our audience, we've had unanimity – does anyone in	
	this audience think that 55 is too old to become a father,	
	would you put your hands up? The entire large audience –	
	one – one young sprite and everyone else in this	5
	audience is overwhelmingly taking the same view as our	
	panellists.	
SW:	Probably almost everybody's 55.	
JD:	I can see many people younger than 55 here. We'll go to	
	our next question please.	10

Aud: Claire Taylor. Would members of the panel enjoy two
        prostitutes living next door to them?
JD: This relates to the proposed change in the law to allow up
        to two prostitutes working together from the same
        building among other changes in the law. Theresa Villiers.   15
                                                              (BBC 2006)

This extract shows a couple of routine but important practices of
definition. The first is common to the television version of the format,
although when it comes to radio broadcasts it is a practice in which the
role of the chair as definer becomes more crucial. In lines 1 through to 7
of the extract, Dimbleby asks for a show of hands in order to produce a
snapshot of the opinion of those in the studio. While members of the
panel are free to intervene with their own view of the result, the chair's
role gives him the power to adjudicate on the poll and define the extent
of audience opinion one way or the other; in this case 'overwhelmingly
taking the same view as our panellists'. Routinely, however, this extends
to the chair's assumption of what we have previously termed the role of
'ventriloquist' for the audience, presuming to speak for the audience's
support or disapproval towards a response by one of the panel. The
capacity of the chair to regulate audience contributions is also in
evidence in a different way in line 13, where Dimbleby places the
question from the audience in context. It is notable that since the
question asked is agreed in advance by the production team, the chair is
accorded the power of interpreting the question within the current news
agenda (Anderson 1999: 65). Again, this involves the chair occupying a
position of expertise on behalf of the audience, in a manner similar to
that discussed in the last chapter, where Dimbleby elaborates on the
immediacy of questions and expresses them in a manner conventional
to the genre.

It is therefore apparent that the programmes proceed on the basis of
a constructed relationship between the position of the chair, the panel
and the assembled public, and the interaction that obtains between
them. One of the key components of this relationship is that this studio
audience should be seen as representative of the political public at large
(McNair et al. 2003: 35) and the dialogue between the panel and the
audience – as mediated by the chairperson – is symbolic of political
involvement across the democratic space. There are also a number of
strategies by which the two programmes lay specific claim to a state-wide
dialogue by building in the participation of the population watching at
home. In *Question Time*, where a relatively similar format is recast for
television, viewers are invited to use their mobile phones and Internet
connections to address pitch their own questions, with the promise that

a member of the panel will be available to read and respond. *Any Questions?* goes much further than this in giving a role to the wider public, and runs a follow-on feedback programme called *Any Answers?* to provide a forum for listeners to phone or email with their views. Although none of the programmes allow for wider public input at the time of broadcast, both strategies serve to highlight the importance of maintaining the mood of public dialogue.

In addition to the discursive arrangements that regulate debate across political public participation programming, Anderson (1999: 94) reflects upon the importance of the physical arrangements of the studio in setting the stage for these mediated enactments of participation. While the very purpose of the studio arrangement is predicated on 'the viewing audience', the studio itself clearly distinguishes between the chair and panellists on the stage and the attending audience. This division between the members of the studio public and those sitting at the top table is built into the foundations of the format. Journalist and critic Jonathan Freedland points out that the very titles *Question Time* and *Any Questions?* imply that the audience is expected to contain itself to requesting answers of those in power, with no expectation that they should come armed with their own policy suggestions (quoted in McNair 2000: 113). It always lies within the power of the chair of the programme to decide whether any contribution is admissible and worthy of a response (McNair 2000: 113), although audience members might demur from the rules of propriety and express a view alien to the political establishment represented on the studio stage, at least until the chair either persuades them to be quiet or the production team decommission nearby microphones.

It should be acknowledged that these programmes are still engaged in generating discussion outside of the studio and across the democratic space (McNair et al. 2002: 412). We have already discussed the follow-up programme *Any Answers?*, where supplementary points are invited and entered into public circulation. Yet, this does not adequately address the question of whether those points raised by the representative publics in public participation programming reflect the concerns of the citizenry as a whole, something politician Shirley Williams highlights in the second extract (line 8). Perhaps the keenest objection to any claim to public representativeness is that the studio audience is self-selected, having been invited to apply for tickets as part of the ritual sign off from a previous week. McNair et al. (2002: 410) note with approval the production team's efforts to maximize diversity in the studio audience, while at the same time acknowledging that those present seem to end up largely 'male, middle class, middle aged and white'.

While it is easy to overplay the demographic deficit between the studio audience for *Question Time* or *Any Questions?* and the electorate outside, it is clear that embodying the political public is not a straightforward matter. There is also a complex relationship between these formats at the governing authorities. Certainly, as Guy Starkey (2007: 135) points out, the format is instrumental in holding the governing party accountable both to the public and to political opponents. Yet the terms of the discussion are discursively constrained by production-led judgements over relevance and political legitimacy. Similar concerns over discursive control will be explored in the next section, which will look at other media formats that draw upon the participating public.

The political public as correspondents: the case of talk radio

In their discussion of public participation media, one of the forms that McNair et al. (2003: 33) identified was that of the 'phone-in debate'. While the regular studio debate is relatively unusual, the phone-in debate is a feature of a number of national media terrains, especially on radio. As McNair et al. point out, the 'radio phone-in' is the term favoured by such programming in the UK, and a number of radio stations such as BBC Radio 5 and *Talk Sport* devote a substantial proportion of their airtime to the format. In Australia, where the genre is known as 'talkback radio', the Radio National programme *Australia Talks Back* runs each weekday at six o'clock Eastern time, and invites callers to discuss around a particular, normally political, theme. However, it is the US, where the format is known as 'talk radio', where the greatest number of programmes is broadcast, and where the culture and political implications of the genre are subject to the most discussion.

Much of the research on the activities of talk radio in particular has emphasized this political dimension. In the US context, where the popularity of right wing talk show hosts such as Rush Limbaugh has prompted a series of studies into talk radio and political influence. The starting point for a number of these studies has been the seeming popularity of talk radio among conservatives and the right wing (Hollander 1997; Hall and Cappella 2002) and their findings have been varied. Some, such as Pan and Kosicki (1997), find that a greater than average level of audience engagement with talk radio tends to coincide with keener political interest, and suggest that the very least talk shows do is provide the means for political dialogue and participation. Others argue that discussion generated through talk radio is proving influential in the formulation of policy (Page and Tannenbaum 1996) and may even have been instrumental in the election of presidents (Lance Holbert 2004). Still other studies, such as that by Jones (1998), have been more dismissive of the political influence of talk radio, arguing that it makes little difference either way.

However, another strand of research, including studies by Yanovitzky and Cappella (2001) and Lee and Cappella (2001), offer a useful insight for our purposes. While they argue that talk shows might have a negligible effect in terms of inspiring political engagement, they find instead high and consistent levels of agreement between the views of the talk show audience and those of the production. While talk shows might not inspire political activity in themselves, they may well bring together like-minded individuals around their favoured programmes. In other words, in providing for relatively cohesive sets of political interests, talk shows may well be complicit in the production of what Warner (2002), albeit in a very different context, termed political counterpublics.

Across the broadcast media, talk show host Rush Limbaugh emerged over the course of the 1990s as one of the main figures in what Jeffrey Scheuer (2001: 49) describes as the 'electronic right'. The extract included below, and which we will go on to examine, is from an edition of Rush Limbaugh's talk radio programme *Open Line Friday,* on the EIB Network, broadcast in July 2004. As we will see, the extract offers a demonstration of this form of political public in action:

RL:	Here's Tony in Tampa. We go to the phones. Welcome,	1
	sir. Nice to have you on the program.	
T:	Hi there, Rush. And megadittos from the west coast.	
RL:	Thank you.	
T:	And I just wanted to say, I've been watching this,	5
	and Joe Lieberman, of – of all people, seems to be the	
	only mainstream, you know, right-thinking Democrat	
	on that panel. He comes off=	
RL:	=No, not – not surprising.	
	He has the – why do you think this guy was the first out	10
	of the Democrat primary?	
T:	Well, you're right. You're right. And now after these	
	comments, I'm just waiting for the Democrats' machine	
	to come and, you know, get rid of him. He says	
	where's the apology for, you know, four guys getting	15
	killed and burned and hung from a bridge? Where's	
	the apology for three thousand Americans getting killed?	
	And it – it's just refreshing to see that. I'm glad that	
	finally somebody came out and said it live in the – in	
	the Senate hearings, so=	20

RL: =Yeah, we – we're preparing some
audio soundbites of Lieberman and his opening remarks
now. He has been consistent on this from the get-go. I
can remember watching speeches Lieberman gave
during the Democrat primaries. And he was rating   25
nothing. Nobody was for Lieberman. He was – because
he understands what this is all about, and he is – he
was taking – in favour of taking positions that
strengthen our cause and strengthen our effort. And I
never forget his concession speech. I guess it was in New   30
Hampshire or whatever it was, somewhere early on
in the primaries. His concession speech was – ['] I'm not
going to stop saying what I think is right. Our party is
making a mistake by underestimating the importance
of the conflict that we find ourselves involved in. And I   35
have tried to alert them ['] – and I'm paraphrasing – [']
and I have tried to speak to it, but they're not
interested in hearing about it [']. And that's exactly
what's going in here. This – this is – nobody can tell me
that the effort on the part of this Senate committee today   40
is about improving or enhancing the war effort. Because
if they were really concerned with that, this wouldn't
be happening this way. I mean, there's a number of ways
to do this without making a show trial out of
it, and attempting to force the Secretary of Defense to   45
resign, and get him out the way, so that you can use the
blood in the water to go after the President. Here's Mark
in Sault Sante Marie, Michigan. Thank you for calling,
you're on Open Line Friday. Hi

M: Thank you for taking my call, Rush. I'm quite shocked   50
and disappointed with you, a strict constitutionalist
and somebody who really looks up to the rule of law,
that you're not outraged about the Geneva Convention
being violated in these many instances. And I think it
all stems from the fact that when Saddam was captured,   55
they showed inhumane pictures of him with lights up
his nose and up his mouth, and those pictures being
released. And it's now – what you're seeing now is a
national consequence of that. It just goes down the
chain of command, saying that this is okay=   60

RL: =Mark. Mark. Mark, you can't possibly
believe this.

M: I believe this.

RL: You can't possibly believe that what's happening now
       is because of the way Saddam was treated when he was   65
       captured?
M: The pictures of Saddam, the inhumane pictures? I mean,
       if you're going to – if you're going to be a=[inaudible]=
R: =Inhumane pictures? He was hiding in   70
       a dirt hole.
M: =[inaudible]=not just pick up and choose when you're
       going to follow the law. And I'm suite shocked and
       disappointed with you, Rush, because you're not outraged
       by the fact that the Geneva Convention has been   75
       violated and that these people are, you know, just=
R: =Mark, I'm
       going to tell you what. When I found out that the Geneva
       Convention's been violated, I may get a little concerned,
       but I don't know all there is to know about it. There's   80
       a lot we don't know about this. And I want to warn
       some of you. Some of you are not going to like it,
       and you're going to be really surprised when you find
       out what I think was really going on here.   84
                                              (Media Matters 2004)

This style of media talk is often characterized by the host talking over and interrupting the contributions of callers, which is indicated here by two parallel lines. What is striking about the extract is how hearty the exchanges of greetings are in comparison to those in the extract from *Any Questions?*. In common with similar talk radio transcripts examined by Tolson (2006: 35), the opening exchanges are relatively unconventional in that no request is issued by the callers to begin their point. Rather, participants are welcomed with the implicit understanding that their admittance into the discursive universe of the format will be sufficient to prime callers to set out their point immediately. These openings also involve a performance of collegiality that is particularly marked in the first of the exchanges, where the caller opens 'Hi there, Rush. And megadittos from the west coast' (line 3). 'Megadittos' has developed into a conventional Limbaugh greeting, conveying an overall agreement with the views associated with the programme, Rush himself and the listening 'dittoheads' (Barrett 2004: 93). It is important to stress that this collegiality is based on a shared political outlook, and what follows is a sequence in which Limbaugh and the caller exchange a series of political claims best exemplified in the loaded designation by the caller of Joe Lieberman as 'the only mainstream, you know, right thinking

Democrat' (lines 6–7). This common political cause is then played out in a pair of rhetorical questions in the middle of Tony's third turn ('Where's the apology for, you know, four guys getting killed and hung from a bridge? Where's the apology for three thousand Americans getting killed?' lines 15–18). What emerges is less an argument than a ritual of political belonging.

It is also important to note the performance of political argumentation in evidence here. As much as an effective political public sphere draws sustenance from new intelligence and politically significant information, Limbaugh mobilizes a vocabulary of disclosure and mock surprise when implying the official distribution of misinformation in lines 80–4 ('And I want to warn some of you ... you're going to be really surprised when you find out what I think was really going on here'). In the main, however, even the pretence of political argument is set aside in favour of the assertion of common purpose. And perhaps the clearest indication of the assumption of a set of shared political beliefs comes in the response to the question by Limbaugh, which surrenders coherence while emphasizing the compulsion to agreement: the host asks 'He has the – why do you think this guy was first out the Democratic primary?' (lines 10–11), to which the caller, assuming a connection with Lieberman's description as 'right thinking' responds not with an answer to the question, but with 'well you're right. You're right' (line 12). The caller therefore submits to the host as the more powerful conversant and arbiter of political truth by treating Limbaugh's contribution as an implicit request for confirmation rather than an open request for information from the caller.

What we see so far is less the development of a political dialogue and more the enactment of shared political interests and understandings. However, this depends on a rigid control over the terms of this political public. Limbaugh's management of the political tenor of the programme comes to the fore when a caller strays away from the implicitly agreed political line, as is the case with Mark's contribution beginning on line 50. Limbaugh's rhetorical response to this call is to question whether the caller sincerely believes what is implied to be a patently absurd position (lines 61, 64). With the exception of Mark's brief response 'I believe this' (line 63), Limbaugh then interjects in each of Mark's turns. As well as questioning whether Mark has faith in his own position (line 61), Limbaugh interjects to dispute one of the terms of Mark's question (line 70) and then to outline his own view, which is the political position that dominates the programme (line 77). This call is also significant in highlighting the prominence of the assumed political covenant between the programme host and the overhearing audience. Mark begins his call by claiming alignment with Limbaugh's political principles, invoking

Limbaugh's attachment to the law and the US Constitution. While the caller tries to use this as a rhetorical strategy to expose what he sees as the inconsistencies in Limbaugh's position, it is significant that this is a scheme that involves a performed occupancy of a position within the political community around Limbaugh's broadcasts.

The exchanges here are also similar to Tolson's (2006: 35) examples such that the host – in this case Rush Limbaugh – has 'the power to terminate the call' with 'a minimal closing exchange', the exercise of which betrays another way in which the boundaries of this political public are established: the construction of the political enemy. As Joanna Thornborrow (2002: 84) points out, talk radio can use unconventional closing sequences to terminate a call to deal with time constraints or, as is the case here, to thwart any further response from the caller. Having already ended Tony's call by introducing the following call from Mark (line 45), the end of Mark's call is then marked by a change in the 'footing' of the presenter (Goffman 1981; O'Keeffe 2006: 67), where the address shifts from Mark to 'some' of the overhearing audience ('I want to warn some of you', line 81). Whereas Anne O'Keeffe (2006) sees this as a strategy for placing callers within an established political discourse and constructing a commonality among listeners, Limbaugh appears to be singling 'some' listeners out as potential dissenters.

Limbaugh's reliance on imagined interlopers among his listeners should not be surprising. According to Benedict Anderson (1991: 7), the imagined community is inherently 'limited': its maintenance every bit as dependent on the construction of the outsider as the agreed practices and beliefs of the insider. As the pioneering work of Hall et al. (1978) into a constructed crisis around 'mugging' as its subsequent construction as a problem of racial integration in the UK media shows, such 'outsiders' have still greater political utility when they are seen to trespass 'our' shared space. Such threat from within the democratic system, especially from liberals, propels Limbaugh's discourse, and provides common cause for formations of public assembled there. Limbaugh's mode of address fractures give dynamism to its own notion of a political public by assuming it always harbours an enemy within.

While he provides an excellent insight into the genre of political talk radio, Limbaugh's reputation precedes him. Scheuer summarizes the contribution of Rush Limbaugh to public discourse thus:

> Limbaugh doesn't engage in reasoned debate or thoughtful commentary. Instead, he is an extraordinarily effective invective machine, a font of name-calling, ridicule, ad hominem argument, context removal, and other offences against critical thinking. Demonizing liberal and media 'elites' in the name of

populism, he mobilises the most intolerant and anti-egalitarian segments of the hate-driven far right.

(Scheuer 2001: 49)

Scheuer's account may not be practising what it implicitly preaches in terms of laying off the name calling, but it nonetheless makes plain how little room for error Limbaugh leaves in expressing his political agenda. Perhaps such media provides a rallying point for the formation of political publics more than they collect political converts. After all, the available research on the composition of Limbaugh's audience suggests that opponents of Limbaugh's vision of the world are likely to have opted to tune into another radio talk show more in keeping with their own beliefs (Lee and Cappella 2001; Yanovitzky and Cappella 2001). Even so, this type of address is essential in invoking the notion of a political public around a platform of public participation, while at the same time asserting the qualities of those members of the political public whose views are contrary to the agreed values of the political community.

Conclusion

In the opening chapter, we reflected upon media's place in contributing to and fashioning networks and practices of governance (Palmer 2003). Dominant elements of the broadcast media, it was postulated, help in instilling forms of behaviour appropriate to the maintenance of an orderly population (Foucault 1991). In this chapter, we have seen how public participation media offers controlled public empowerment, positioning those involved within clearly determined relations of power, as particular forms of political subject. Although we have looked at the construction of the participative political public as a means of governance, what we see are certainly forms of public activity that equate with the exercise of political force. In the case of political participation programming in the UK, this imperative of extending empowerment is built into the conduct of the programmes, such that the gathered public are guided in their encounters with the political elite, in terms of both their style of questioning and how best to signal their approval or otherwise of any answers they receive. As McNair et al. (2003: 67) derive from their discussions with the producers of *Question Time*, 'the ideal public participant, like the ideal panellist, is someone with a clear view, able to articulate it effectively'.

However, while this mode of conduct is intended to strengthen the position of the public participant, it is worth noting how it also requires them to regulate their actions according to established political norms not of their making: 'the rules of engagement', as McNair et al. style them. We noted that the regulation of political expression is aided by the distribution of participants around the studio as well as by the rules of discussion. Scannell (1991: 6) argues that such arrangements, in concert with other semiotic factors, are central to understanding the structures of political power: 'the design, layout and lighting of the studio; the age, appearance, sex and dress of participants' all offer 'warrantable inferences about the nature of the event'. In the radio debate *Any Questions?* the public are seated in banks of seats, facing the chair and the elite participants; a division between public and policy makers that is intensified in the televised format by a row of cameras. To some extent, therefore, public political participation is offered within a prevailing discourse of political engagement, and political and cultural authority.

On the other hand, we found that this was far from the only form of political public participation available, and that others were less formal and conventional in tone. Talk radio formats, such as that represented by Rush Limbaugh, mark out their territory by eschewing conventional political discourse and what are routinely presented there as the special interests of formal politics and politicians. However, these programmes have their own terms of public participation, which construct their terms of legitimacy in representing the public. Specifically, such programmes demand that participants submit to those political ideas that motivate the agenda of the programme. In other words, there is a form of public participation, represented in talk radio, that often eschews conventional political discourse, but in which participation is within carefully policed ideological parameters. In terms of where this leaves the political public, talk radio exemplifies the artful division of the political public into competing groups, but seeks to admit only those sectors that represent a given set of political interests.

Questions for discussion

- How would you design a public discussion on politics for broadcast? Giving due consideration to the limits and require-ments of the various media platforms, do you consider that freedom of expression should take precedence over orderliness and structure?
- What advantages do Internet-based forums hold over public participation broadcasting, and what limitations do they bring?

Further reading

McNair, B., Hibberd, M. and Schlesinger, P. (2003) *Mediated Access.*
    Luton: Luton University Press.
Scheuer, J. (2001) *The Sound Bite Society.* New York: Routledge.

5 The construction of the cultural public

Introduction

In the opening chapter we summarized some of the ways in which constructions of the public are played out in media. These included public service media and the arrangements that underpin public participation across a number of media forms. It was argued that these represented varying conceptions of public, each geared towards serving different political and cultural interests and policy agendas. In this chapter we will begin to explore the usefulness of distinguishing between political and cultural configurations of public. Certainly, the entangled relations between culture and politics complicate any such conceptual division. Indeed, there have reminders of the articulation of the two all through the previous chapters, where practices around the political public undergo cultural transformations, such as we witnessed in the development of community jargon in talk radio. We anticipated the combination of political and cultural influences in Chapter 2, when we discussed the consumerization of the political public sphere by techniques and practices of marketing. In this chapter, we now look to the development of the cultural public: at its emergence in the era of industrialization, and its relationship with systems of difference and hierarchies of judgement.

Culture as a form of politics

In *The Fall of Public Man*, Richard Sennett (2002: 89) claims that the mores of public life are an expression of the division between nature and culture, amounting to the practice of upholding 'certain basic rights' above the raw force of instinct. As half of an affected and multifaceted opposition, it is no surprise that 'culture' carries a complex of meanings. Something of the range of this diversity is reflected in the many activities and approaches included under the academic rubric of 'cultural studies', the key texts of which are drawn from such diverse academic subjects as philosophy, anthropology and literary studies. According to Chris Barker

(2003: 5), it is an attention to 'power' that provides the common concern to set cultural studies apart from the disciplines upon which it draws, and in particular alertness towards the use of representation in how power is exercised. As part of an attitude to social relations that has come to be known as 'cultural politics', networks of power are seen to be integrated into everyday life. Importantly, culture and the institutional practices and discourses of formal politics are not synonymous, and Paul Gilroy (2000: 283) reflects on the capacity of culture to operate against the forces and strictures of the political realm.

There are, however, even more fundamental variations in the meanings of culture to be found in common parlance. In one of the texts cultural studies was later to deploy, Raymond Williams (1961: 41–2) sets out three general patterns behind the use of 'culture'. In some contexts, culture is used to refer to the expressive development in the road to some 'state or process of human perfection', invoking a system of evaluation we will elaborate upon later. On other occasions, culture offers a proper description of the archive of a civilization: that sum of documents and artefacts represented as evidencing and memorializing a set of qualities and shared values. In terms of the representation of these relationships, the mass media has played a prominent role in articulating 'particular traditions' with popular practices and beliefs, and presenting the combination as symbolic towards the progress of a given civilisation. Both of these qualities inform Williams' third definition of culture as the socially significant system of 'meanings and values not only in art and learning but also in institutions and ordinary behaviour'. In all three senses, to differing extents, culture is a quality that can be aspired to and can be surmised, in contexts ranging from the public assessment of merit in art (Budd 1996: 1) to domestic rules governing eating practices (Levi-Strauss [1964] 1992: 241).

While sharing Raymond Williams' concern with 'the particular traditions and societies' of cultural engagement (Williams 1961: 41), Jim McGuigan (2004: 9) warns that tolerance of too broad a definition of culture, particularly in its association with everyday activities of self-actualization, lets in the limiting assumption that 'everything is culture'. Rather, McGuigan (2004: 12) asserts the need to make purposeful distinctions between forms of culture. Nick Couldry (2000), for example, advises that complexities of understanding, motive and intent are such that we can more productively think of a multiplicity of *cultures*, even within a confined social environment. This alertness to difference is all the more important, argues McGuigan, since cultures set the boundaries and provide the rationales for division and systematic exclusion (McGuigan 2004: 9). While Raymond Williams (1981: 12) would place a greater emphasis on 'social order' in comprehending culture,

McGuigan is still more explicit in calling attention to the role of social control and the role of culture in supporting the 'economic reason' necessary to modern capitalism.

It should therefore be clear that the distinction that we make between the political and cultural forms of media public is not intended as an implicit claim that the political and the cultural have no reciprocal dealings. On the contrary, cultural activities and the systems of meanings that they generate both express and help to reproduce politically charged practices of social inclusion, exclusion, self-definition and the definition of others, and the media has a key role in all of these processes. Instead, 'the cultural public' is intended to focus attention on those formations of public that have emerged and developed outside of the formal political realm of electoral engagement and discussions of policy direction and implementation. As will become plain in the chapters to come, cultural publics have political consequences in that they provide the organizing principles behind the exercise of everyday power and governance. What's more, we will see that issues germane to formal politics arise and are debated in media formats routinely considered to be outside the remit of the political public sphere. The distinction we draw is therefore between the formations of public that gather around the activities of formal, democratic politics – which we have looked at over the last three chapters – and those constructs of public to emerge within media concerned with the broader cultural realm.

The roots of the cultural public

In a discussion of its emergence in the US, Bernard Cohen (1963) argues that the contemporary cultural public developed during the latter part of the nineteenth century in parallel with the acceleration of technology and processes of urbanization. The reasons for this coincidence of forces are determinedly commercial, and is said to have had destructive consequences for the prominence of what we have described as the political public. The extra investment and running costs necessary for new printing technologies could no longer be met through the subscription of a specialist audience, leaving a shortfall that had to be covered by advertising revenue. This meant that newspapers aspiring to a share of this growing urban market had to compete for a more expansive audience base 'by including in one inexpensive paper all the subjects and features that separate audiences had hitherto found in specialized publications' (Cohen 1963: 248). Cohen (1963: 249) suggests that this revenue driven expansion of the reading public had implications for what was demanded of the audience, claiming that 'the special interests of special readers were substantially lost in the adaptation of the newspaper to the interests, standards and pastimes of a mass public that was lightly educational and in the market for diversion and amusement'.

Although Henrik Örnebring (2007) describes a similar set of developments in the European context, hostile to specialization and in favour of anodyne mass-marketing, Erich Auerbach (1973) argues that emergent shared cultural practices proved more significant than industrialization and commerce. Auerbach identifies the emergence in Europe of a 'literary public', recognizable by an interest in the arts over politics. He also credits this culturally driven public with a more substantial heritage than those described by Cohen and Örnebring, citing roots in the latter days of the Roman republic and learned traditions set by such figures as the statesman and orator Cicero. Importantly, Auerbach offers an idea of public that extends beyond the confines of the politically enfranchised: a cultural formation shifting away from the wealthy and traditionally educated to incorporate the wider, literate population, with fewer limitations on gender and class (Auerbach 1973: 419). Of course, there were forces other than a shared yearning for the brilliance of Cicero driving this emergent public. Auerbach points to a high level of childlessness in upper class families, allowing a greater concentration on matters outside of the domestic sphere. Yet, for all these extended terms of inclusion, it remains that admission to this cultural public would be governed by access to formal education at some level, where the relatively 'fluid' relationship between the cultural public and the 'people' at large would be governed by standards of literary and cultural know-how.

Of course, where media industries are concerned, the economic draw of the popular is a powerful one. Kevin Williams (1998) notes that while the development of a 'quality' sector allowed distinctions to remain in place, what had been a range of 'newspapers, journals and periodicals appealing to different slices of life' in the late eighteenth century, turned within the space of a hundred or so years to 'a highly capitalised market product' (Williams 1998: 23, 49). Yet it remains that the relationships between culture and economic class are multifarious, and exploitative in quite unexpected ways. In an examination of the development of the nineteenth century music hall, for example, John Storey (2003: 10–12) describes how moneyed intellectuals used the platforms of learned journals and societies to separate out the 'folk music' of the rural working class – giving it connotations of authenticity and whole-someness – from the supposedly superficial and depraved 'music hall' favoured by the urban workforce. These practices placed educated distaste for particular types of music within the armoury of class prejudice. Although the relationship has never been a simple one in which elite groups wield regulatory power over working class tastes (see Stedman Jones 1982), the rise of the cultural public coincides with the introduction of media forms to the working classes.

The cultural public and judgement

A central strand in the development of cultural forms of public has been their configuration around various recreational pursuits and lifestyle choices. While some have argued that a process of fragmentation in the political terrain has latterly given rise to a number of political counter-publics (Warner 2002), hierarchies and distinctions are part of the very definition of the cultural public, such that different categories of public are formed and reproduced through participation in various forms of cultural activity. We can easily see the benefits of this for cross-cultural influence and diversity, and just as dispute propels the political public forward, a similar dynamic of difference may be said to benefit the cultural public. Yet, while there may be a complex and often veiled relationship between political publics and traditional social hierarchies, there are much clearer regimes of judgement exercised within the cultural realm. Such judgements are certainly associated with cultural 'elitists' such as British philosopher Roger Scruton (2005), who would have us all believe that some cultural forms are inherently superior to others, so that the publics of production and consumption are divisible according to the innate quality of the culture in which they have an interest. While these assumptions have been subject to prolonged critique within cultural studies (Frith [1991] 2006), they nonetheless retain considerable purchase in public discourse on and within the cultural realm, and are apparent in the distribution of awards for achievement in culture and the arts (Street 2005b).

Before we come to examine the implications of cultural forms of media public, it would be useful to use this section to examine the root assumptions that structure discussion of the cultural public within the universities and beyond. The foundations of these regimes of cultural judgement lie within the arguments made in Matthew Arnold's ([1869] 1933)*Culture and Anarchy*. While written in the nineteenth century and pertaining to the relatively embryonic cultural publics referred to in the previous section, Kenneth Dyson (1996: 18) argues that Arnold's continuing relevance to media analysis stems from his determination to link judgements over culture with core ethical and aesthetic values: in other words, to make culture a public issue. Rather than setting apart high and low forms of culture, Arnold is concerned with promoting culture per se as the path to human development. For Arnold, culture should be pure and uplifting, and he despises those who deploy culture for the ends of self-aggrandizement (the sorts of collective social practices we will describe when we come to discuss Pierre Bourdieu). Such people debase culture, reducing it to 'an engine of social and class distinction, separating its holder, like a badge or title, from other people who have not got it' (Arnold [1869] 1933: 43). Arnold's champions are those devoted to the essential task of encouraging cultural enlightenment, and so helping in the augmentation of a cultural public of a very particular kind.

There is, however, another body of thinking, exemplified by the school of thought gathered round F. R. Leavis (Samson 1992). According to Thomas Osborne (2003), the boldness of Leavis's approach has left the critic a peripheral and divisive figure in his own discipline of literary studies and beyond. Yet, Osborne (2003: 518) argues, Leavis embodies the tradition of emphasizing literature as an object, rather than focusing on the practices of reading and interpretation. Furthermore, David Macey (2000: 225) suggests that Leavis is known both for helping transform the study of literature from a 'gentlemanly conversation' to pedagogical practice, and for expressing and establishing a set of dominant assumptions on cultural merit. Osborne (2003: 517) explains Leavis's nevertheless tenuous place in the academic history of cultural critique by describing his writing as 'too good to follow, yet too embarrassing to emulate'.

It is Leavis's suggestion that hierarchies of legitimacy and substance are integral to culture. He agrees with Arnold that solace can be found in elevated forms of art, literature and other media, but insists the great majority of the population have scant regard or appreciation for these higher forms of culture, foregoing substantial and informative news coverage, for example, to read newspapers based on entertainment and salacious gossip (Leavis 1948: 143n). The production and maintenance of a superior culture therefore depends upon a small and discerning sector of the public: an avant garde that are intuitively able to distinguish good culture from bad, and are themselves in a position to produce culture in its finer form. These elite are assisted by a sector of willing lieutenants in a second sector of the cultural public. Also in a minority but at least capable of being coached into recognizing and appreciating good quality culture (Leavis 1948: 143), this second division routinely seek 'guidance' from the cultural sections of high quality newspapers (Leavis 1948: 159).

The Leavisite view of the state of the cultural public is characterized by a thoroughgoing pessimism. Leavis sees whatever examples there are of an intelligent and discerning culture as under the threat of what he describes as the 'psychological Gresham Law' that 'primitive feelings and impulses' will tend to win out against motives of artistic integrity and rationality (Leavis 1948: 148). The free market of culture is therefore an inherently destructive force, allowing the majority of its consumers to restrict themselves to culture of the lowest hue, and designed to facilitate self-delusion. So long as this insidious relationship between culture, marketing and apparent choice holds the upper hand, it is easy to offer a series of seductively lazy options while claiming, as early UK newspaper baron Lord Northcliffe does, that one is merely 'giving the public what it wants' (Leavis 1948: 148). Leavis is keen therefore that we should envision the cultural public as separable according to levels of insight and discretion, with precedence given to the tastes and preferences of the minority elite.

For the affiliation of Marxist critics and theorists in the Frankfurt School, it was not the supposedly depraved instincts of the working classes that blocked the development of culture, but a strategic alliance of industry and state concerns. In a classic essay on 'the culture industry', Theodor Adorno and Max Horkheimer ([1944] 1979: 121) insist that while it might appear as though mass produced culture is designed to sate the appetites of its audience, it is actually driven by the economic imperatives of the capitalist state. The culture industry is dedicated to standardizing mass recreation according to a series of subject positions predetermined by the capitalist system: 'the public is catered for with a range of mass produced products of varying quality' and 'everybody must behave (as if spontaneously) in accordance with his previously determined and indexed level, and choose the category of mass product turned out for his type' (Adorno and Horkheimer [1944] 1979: 123). In what Horkheimer ([1941] 1982) describes as the erosion of the free-thinking individual subject, the culture industry provides distraction and recuperation for the late capitalist worker, while foisting upon them an artificial type of culture whose formulas and clichés forbid reflective engagement (Adorno and Horkheimer [1944] 1979: 136). The cultural public to emerge is best a social collective designed to engender delusion and is at worst an instrument of economic oppression and alienation.

In *Inventing Popular Culture*, John Storey (2003: 30–1) suggests that a common factor uniting the reactionary criticism of Leavis with the Marxism of the Frankfurt School is their shared vision of culture as divisible between the authentic, high or pure on the one hand, and the fake, low or sullied on the other. Granted, the Leavisites see mass culture as a cause of cultural, moral and intellectual ruin, whereas the Marxists see it as an instrument of political oppression. Albeit with different consequences, both also see this as a division transferring directly onto the cultural public, so that a minority demonstrate tastes and engage in cultural practices of inherently greater value than the rest. Moreover, in spite of the application of such cultural values to contemporary broadcasting (see Scruton 2005), Dyson (1996: 19) argues that the brute system of cultural value demanded by Leavis becomes exponentially more difficult to sustain in a multiplatform, multigeneric, code driven media environment; a point directed against Marxism in McNair's (2006) discussion of 'cultural chaos', having been conceded earlier by Leo Lowenthal (1961: 12). For one thing, many of those characteristics that make for successful television – an emphasis on mediated sociability, the stress of the visual, emotional engagement (Scannell 1996) – run contrary to the practices of sober reflection demanded by Leavis and offer the very distractions despised by the Frankfurt School (Adorno 1957). Second, the use of what Paddy Scannell (1996) calls 'mediated sociability' varies from genre to genre, such that any appraisal of news content would differ in its expectations of quality from a discussion of a panel show, making it difficult to conceive of a common vocabulary of productive criticism. Both critiques also leave little room for the discussions around 'balance, variety and audience appeal' raised by multigeneric scheduling for a disparate audience (Dyson 1996: 19).

It is John Corner's position that many of these difficulties lie in the prejudicial interpretations of the relationship between problematic notions of the popular – so far, implicitly disparaged by both the Leavisites and the Frankfurt School – and the equally difficult idea of the public. Of the popular and the public, Corner (2001: 152–3) writes that 'the various ways of placing the media as objects of study have been influenced in their formation not only by the nature of the perceived relationship between the two – at times one of virtual synonymity, often of tension and occasionally of mutual exclusion – but by the continuing problems to which each term itself gives rise'. The development of the popular – both empowering and problematic in its capacity to define and condemn simultaneously – has been summarized in a well-known essay by Stuart Hall (1981). However, it certainly remains the case that the development of the popular as an academic concern has provided critics of media studies with a weapon with which to beat the discipline (Corner 1998: 167–79).

Even within media and cultural analysis, Jim McGuigan (1992) and Greg Philo and David Miller (2001) identify strands of media studies that they see as assuming uncritical acceptance of popular power, and that seek to make a case for audience members' capacity to make their own judgements on media texts, and to utilize them in creative and enfranchising ways. Philo and Miller target what they see as an undue elevation of the domestic sphere in a way that presents the pleasures and politics of the household with an undeserved significance, without sufficient regard to the broader economic context of consumption, best reflected in the rise of lifestyle television genres and their study. Parallel dilemmas arise in the interpretation of 'popular' consumption as forms of political engagement, as with Cardo and Street's (2007) study linking the activities and practices of the reality TV show *Vote For Me* with the attitudes and procedures of citizenship and political participation. While this is partly an issue of fashioning reading practices for media genres, the stakes of this dispute are perhaps higher when the issues at risk are matters of shared consequence: what we might loosely term 'public discourse'.

As we will recall from Chapter 1, the ambivalences behind 'the public' are every bit as acute, but debates around the public become all the more charged when juxtaposed with the popular. In such contexts, Corner sees commonly held notions of the public as invested with the sorts of Leavisite instincts to judge and exert cultural control. Picking up on a line of attack prevalent in media studies, Corner points out how much the public is seen as gendered, forming part of what Joke Hermes (1997) sees as the imposition of a set of normative, masculine values. To put this objection another way, the public forms part of what feminist linguistics describes as a lexicon designed to facilitate the consolidation of male power (Cameron 1992). Yet, as Corner (2001: 156) points out, other critics equally attuned to feminist values would prefer to extend and improve upon the application of public in a way that demands a more honest commitment to what he describes as a 'public system informed by public values' (see, for example, Livingstone 2005a).

The definition of the popular that informs much worthwhile scholarship is therefore skewed by the circumstances of its own development. Corner suggests that the retreat of the term 'ideology' from the critical agenda, in particular, has allowed media audience studies to develop free from the need to consider institutional power or of an obligation to consider the economic imperatives of media production. Accordingly, while a broader account is offered than some of the critics admit, the balance has shifted too far towards audience freedom, creativity and empowerment. The development of the public, Corner argues, has been every bit as unhelpful. Much of the current use of the public has drawn upon a set of ill defined normative values. Such values have developed in a way that elides the history of publicness as a mechanism for exercising arbitrary control and are applied without thinking through both the limits and characteristics of citizenship (see Palmer 2003). What is needed, according to Corner, is a fresh orientation of public that shows a commitment to democratic citizenship and can invite and build upon a productive relationship with a realistic vision of the popular. In the next section, we will begin to unpack some of the complex strategies of empowerment and self-definition behind this series of relationships.

The cultural public and practices of distinction

To examine some of the implications for power and governance in these systems of cultural selection, we can turn to the work of sociologist Pierre Bourdieu. Bourdieu (1984) asserts that the divisions of taste and judgement between forms of culture are relatively arbitrary, and are kept in place for the purposes of fashioning and then justifying systems of social 'distinction' and preferment. For Garnham and Williams (1986: 17), Bourdieu represents 'a frontal assault upon all essentialist theories of cultural appropriation (taste) and cultural production (creativity), upon all notions of absolute, universal cultural values'. In practical terms, this relativist stance throws into peril the dominant role hitherto accorded to the intelligentsia and championed by Leavis. Bourdieu takes the view that it is· not the inherent qualities of culture that demarcates and establishes the hierarchy of credentials in any cultural public. Rather, social power resides in the capacity to define cultural practices for the purposes of lionizing the activities and tastes of certain groups as evidence of a greater legitimacy, competence and capacity for insight.

While the apportionment of judgement may be arbitrary, the framework within which these distinctions are exercised is not. Bourdieu argues that this system of cultural dominance is secured by the construction of three formations of taste: legitimate, middlebrow and popular. While legitimate taste is the preserve of the highly education, objects and forms designated as 'popular' are, according to Bourdieu (1984: 16), 'most frequent among the working classes'. It is, according to Bourdieu, through their knowledge of and engagement in these categorizations of taste that the middle and educated classes continue to secure their position relative to the lower classes, such that practices of consumption constructed around notions of cultural merit are mobilized as tools of division. Furthermore, Bourdieu argues, the taste of the dominant classes is given its undue legitimacy through such state apparatuses as the education system and the arts funding boards. And because legitimate taste is accepted as the pre-eminent form, being able to demonstrate competence in this – possession of what Bourdieu calls 'cultural capital' – enables interaction and movement within a more esteemed and influential social environment.

The link between this cultural capital and the education system does produce some fluidity in the composition and size of these more venerated sectors of the cultural public – admitting the best educated of the lower classes – meaning that the distribution of cultural capital has an influence on the overall make-up of the cultural field (Bourdieu 1996: 127). However, it is important to emphasize that cultural capital amounts to training in society proprietary, and so is more attuned to governing conduct within the cultural public than extending social influence to the disempowered. Overall, the important factor is that this dominant form of taste and consumption has no objective claim to legitimacy or to greater worth, but rather it is a means for the practices of already dominant social groups to dominate over others.

While his focus is on the print-based mediums of news and popular literature, Gramsci (1995: 206–10) notes that one of the chief means of aligning the national–popular with the hegemonic interests of the day is through mass media – mainly by forging a 'sentimental connection' between the intellectual leaders and the public (Gramsci 1971: 418). Yet, while echoes of popular empowerment run through Gramsci's writings, we should remember that his position is fundamentally one that stresses the importance of economic factors in understanding culture. While Gramsci (1971: 182) stresses that concessions of an economic nature must routinely be offered to maintain popular support, he also argues that the cultivation of a 'national–popular' – where the interests of the dominant group are successfully aligned with a sense of national destiny – goes hand-in-hand with the need to develop the working classes and peasantry as a 'market' (Gramsci 1995: 256). Thus, there is considerable state interest in defining a public and according it cultural leadership, but the resulting cultural formation remains answerable to the economic imperatives of the state.

The cultural public and the politics of representation

As the accounts outlined above have shown, even those constructions of the public seemingly outside of the political realm are infused with political and cultural significance. How does this unfold in the management of the relationship between public and media? On the one hand, political and other forms of categorization are used in the development of media content, manifest in media genres. Also, divisions of forms of public allow the maintenance of regimes of taste and discernment that produce elite forms of public, both in the cultural and the formal political arenas. In this way, media publics have become tools of definition and control for those in positions of political and cultural domination. On the other hand, the non-political realm has hierarchies of taste and prestige of its own, and engages in its own struggles of representation. We can see this concern with culture over formal politics in the writing of Leavis. While his ideas have political implications (Storey 1985), Leavis is not in the business of telling us to spend more time campaigning and otherwise participating in party politics. Rather, Leavis's concern is with encouraging what he sees as discretion in cultural activities within terms that he would approve.

It is with this distinction between the cultural and formal–political realms in mind that John Hartley (1992) seeks to rescue notions of the 'popular' in talk of the media public by emphasizing the role of media texts themselves. To Hartley (1992: 24), politically motivated approaches such as those of the Marxist tradition and to a lesser extent cultural studies are ill suited to the study of collectives, on the basis that they default to a view of the public as 'masses' and so 'passive, depoliticised, and in need of organization' (Hartley 1992: 84). Better that we search for broader forms of public based on cultures of textual practice than continuing to search forlornly for amorphous clusters of political agents. Since the replacement of the city state by broader, nation-based forms of government, Hartley argues that the public exists in and through media, and emerges through particular practices of representation. Accordingly, instead of the various correspondences and gaps 'between individuals and audiences', we ought to think about how 'the connection between the individual and the social' is read within a broader textual regime of publicness (Hartley 1992: 85). These would include such strategies as that which Horton and Wahl (1982) describe as the 'para-social interactional' media performance of conversation and intimacy with the audience, and what Scannell (1996) describes above as 'mediated sociability'. In sharp contrast to the concerns raised by Lippmann ([1922] 1997) over the legitimacy of the media public, Hartley sees little relevance in whether this mediated public corresponds to 'reality' by social scientific standards. Instead, Hartley (1992: 21) argues that the 'apparatus of reality construction' is so pervasive as to have produced a textually driven 'popular reality' within which substantial cultural publics may operate.

There are two main components to understanding the cultural public in Hartley's vision. The first is its relative detachment from the established mores of assessing political engagement, which Hartley asserts merely serve to exercise systems of surveying performance that Foucault (1991), Rose (1999) and Palmer (2003) describe as 'governance' over the cultural public. Whereas the classically conceived political public sees differences are resolved in the name of maintaining an orderly and productive civil realm, the realm of the cultural public is one in which differences are highlighted and celebrated (Hartley 1992: 2). Hartley situates this predominance of cultural over formal politics within the context of the end of the Cold War in the 1980s and the subsequent retreat of 'the left' as a vehicle of substantial political dispute (Hartley 1992: 15). While many have noted that the subsequent attacks of 9/11 exposed the complacency of Francis Fukayama's (1992) proliberal 'end of history' thesis, much of the discourse around the threat of terrorism draws upon the preservation of culture and civilization rather than political ideas. As Tariq Ali (2002) points out, the emergent discourses of defence and attack seek to justify political action on the basis of religious fundamentalist beliefs on both sides – in particular, extreme examples of Christian and Muslim doctrine. In the case of the liberal-democratic West, the conceit of military aggression motivated by a concern to 'spread democracy' (Hobsbawm 2007: 115), is presented as a way of defending a form of culture, routinely cited as an inherently national 'way of life', which is aggregated with a liberal view of civil public culture.

The second set of factors in understanding Hartley's conception of popular public are the assumptions behind the division between public and private. Hartley (1992: 35) argues that the telling difference between the place of the public in classical politics and now is that, rather than electing political elites to work on a mandate, the classical arrangement invited all citizens to participate in core political activities. This gave rise to an opposition between public and private at variance with the one that we see now, such that matters of state and shared concern formed a part of everyday discussion, and were integrated with domestic selfhood in a way that is now less likely. There was, Hartley writes, a sense in which the classical 'private' figured only as a derisory byword for ignorance of collective responsibility (Hartley 1992: 39): a stigma that feminist theorists in particular still see in the image of the feminized household (Martin and Mohanty 1988). However, Hartley argues, in the emergent conception of significant political action, the emphasis has gone the other way. While the public realm is concerned with bureaucracy and the management of policy, the private realm, in a way that will become clear in the chapters to come, has become a preferred arena in which authenticity is married with public action (Hartley 1992: 35).

There is also an important variation in the dynamic of Hartley's media public, which draws upon its conceptual setting. While the activities of the political public are assumed to be propelled by a cultural environment founded on the deliberative democracy, modelled variously on the debating chamber or coffee salon, the cultural public emerges from what Hartley calls the 'mediasphere'. In Hartley's *Popular Reality*, the mediasphere is defined not as a virtual forum of debate as we might characterize the public sphere, but as 'the world of the readership' (Hartley 1996: 122). This tackles head-on the problems raised by

Raymond Williams' (1961) definition of culture as a fixed canon of resources, by widening its embrace to all that is circulating among the occupants of the mediasphere. This would include material and virtual, popular moods as well as public pronouncements, and digital culture as much as the printed word. Hartley seeks to place this sympathetically conceived cultural public in an internally dynamic symbolic environment, characterized by movement and change rather than purpose and tradition.

Certainly, Hartley concedes limits to this site of representation, expression and discussion, in that this mediasphere moves within what Yuri Lotman calls the 'semiosphere'; the overarching 'semiotic space' inherently limited by such factors as linguistic competence and technological and auditory capacity (Hartley 1996: 106). This drive to freedom, however, is fuelled by the terms of participation. Hartley argues that the ethos of the French Revolution set the tone for an ever-developing mode of radical journalism. This has been a form of media performance that has a disregard for ceremonial rule, and is dedicated to chipping away at the foundations of formal political discourse. The iconoclasm of this approach has also enabled it to make full use of the expressive resources of the semiosphere, fashioning a new aesthetic, still modernist and purposeful at root, but 'full of desire, emotion, visuality, kissing' (Hartley 1996: 127).

An overstress on the vitality of the cultural public, however, leaves open all of those questions raised by Bourdieu (1984) on the place of social and political power. As Gareth Palmer (2003) points out, even more than the integration of a market-based ethos, systems of governance in media are sustained in discursive practice. The previous two chapters reflected upon such systems, looking at the expressive hierarchies of political discussion. Hartley, though, is keen to follow Foucault's lead in concentrating on the networks and exchanges of power, rather than seeing power as the exercise of dominance of the institution over the individual. Rather, then, than take our lead from those studies of Foucault's looking at discursive environments based on obligation, such as prisons and hospitals (Foucault 1973; Foucault 1977), Hartley (1992: 86) suggests we concentrate on how 'television's institutional power relations are constantly worked out on both sides of the screen'. This offers the more rounded assessment of broadcasting, amidst a complex of other media platforms, as well as within the context of everyday conversation and domestic relations, all of which bring problems for those seeking to understand in advance the place of media in exercising power within intricate social settings. Yet, as Hartley points out, any renewed focus on context should consider how, even in a multichannel digital context, an increase in 'cultural resources' often amounts to a simple menu of preferred consumption practices, albeit set against the increasingly informed use of broadcasting as a 'cultural resource' (Hartley 1992: 87).

A cultural public sphere

To what extent, then, can we talk of a cultural public sphere? As we have pointed out, there is a broad acknowledgement that the relationship between the political and cultural forms of public, in terms of practice and intension, is a fluid one. However useful these distinctions might be for understanding the different formations of public produced by media, these must be subject to continual dispute and redefinition. Whereas Hartley has just argued that emergent, popular forms of public are better suited to the contemporary social and political environment, Rainey insists that Habermas's public sphere always had a hand in cultural affairs, impacting in an instrumentalist way on the regimes of distinction we've just discussed. Rainey (1998: 5) uses the term 'public culture' as what he calls a 'colloquial counterpart' to the Habermasian political public sphere. This 'institutional counterspace' of public culture is, according to Rainey, every bit as competitive and potentially exclusionary as the most pessimistic version of the public sphere; 'a divided world of patronage, collecting, speculation, and investment'. Staeheli and Mitchell (2004: 147) too, while acknowledging the capacity of the cultural space to provide the 'negative freedoms' of non-interference, warn that this empowerment is curtailed by 'long-standing social practices' of containment, especially as they relate to women in the domestic setting (2004: 155). So while the cultural realm may be less beholden to the mores of formal politics, other conventions fill any void.

It is Jim McGuigan, though, who outlines what we can call a 'cultural public sphere'. Rather than an explicit focus on the relationship between public and private, McGuigan (2005: 429) suggests that the differences between this cultural realm and the political one beloved of Habermas and his followers are of intention and function: the political public sphere sees its place as discussing matters of state, while cultural public spheres are clustered around literature and the arts. In this way, McGuigan's distinction therefore differs from Staeheli and Mitchell's (2004) division between political and private/domestic spheres, as well as those of Warner (2002) or Johansson (2007) between dominant and counter or alternative publics. However, McGuigan relates how even within the literary realm, the cultural public sphere often assumes an informal political role to devastating effect. Voltaire, McGuigan reminds us, penned the novella *Candide* as an 'attack on both religion and uncritical rationalism' for their foolhardy interference in matters of public importance. Indeed, dealing with the transcendent ideas and universal ethics behind the expression of the political, the longevity of the products of the cultural sphere offer a greater and more sustained resonance than, say, the immediate but passing implications of a news story or policy pronouncement – a point reinforced by Christina Slade's (2002: 86) analysis of the 'discourse ethics' of soap opera. By way of example, McGuigan (2005: 430) points to those arguments that popular television forms such as the soap opera can give a more insightful account of the prevalent socio-economic conditions than the most worthy newspaper editorial. Cornel Sandvoss (2007) too, looks at how online discussion of sport routinely develops into exchanges on such political matters as race, gender and national and regional identity, albeit that the partisan style of fan talk often predominates over rational dialogue. Most compellingly of all, McGuigan highlights the determination of the most self-satisfied and dictatorial political regimes to coopt and define artistic merit (McGuigan 2005: 431). Even in liberal, democratic political regimes, arrangements built around public service provide airspace and production costs for such politically engaged output as the progressive drama that emerged from the UK in the 1960s and 1970s. In the very development of public service broadcasting, a concept we looked at in Chapter 1, Michael Bailey (2007) highlights the friction in the development of BBC policy between those content to allow broadcasting to reflect popular expression and the ultimately prevalent forces of 'cultural enlightenment' and governance.

McGuigan argues for a broad cultural public sphere based upon 'the articulation of politics, public and the personal, as a contested terrain through affective (aesthetic and personal) modes of communication'. The purpose of any cultural public should therefore be the generation of discussion rather than the focus and restriction of dialogue towards predetermined ends. To develop in line with dominant consumption practices, any cultural public should extend beyond the 'serious' art genres to include 'the various channels and circuits of mass-popular culture and entertainment' (McGuigan 2005: 435). It is necessary to keep in mind, however, that these channels and circuits inform legitimate cultural practices and aspirations. Thus, we have those forms of judgement and self-policing cultivated by reality programmes such as the television franchise *Big Brother* and daytime make-over shows, described variously as 'modern morality tales' by McGuigan (2005: 236) and modern day 'Pilgrim's Progresses' by Brenda Weber (2005: para. 19).

So what are the dominant forms of activity within these cultural public spheres? McGuigan identifies three types of attitude: the first of which he describes as 'uncritical populism'. This is the position that culture in the mass media age is inherently democratic, such that the consuming public are free to browse the alternatives in an open market and so are the compilers of their own cultural menus (McGuigan 2005: 436). There is some affinity here with the position, outlined in Chapter 2, of those who advocate a marketing approach to political communication (Lees-Marshment 2004). The second attitude of 'radical subversion' holds that the most effective means of engaging with the cultural terrain is to act as a cultural naysayer and to attack all dominant media forms as tools of the oppressors, and to produce in their place a homemade counter-cultural response, occasioning a temporary systemic upset, in parallel with direct strategies of demonstration and disruption (McGuigan 2005: 437). Historic examples of radical subversion would have included the early Gay Pride marches, and would now include the activities of many of the anticapitalist and anarchist movements. The third position of 'critical intervention' seeks to harness the pragmatism of uncritical populism while retaining the conscience and idealism of radical subversion (McGuigan 2005: 438). This approach sets out to persuade the system to change from within, according to its own terms. McGuigan points to examples such as the establishment of the fund raising 'telethon', and we might include such politically motivated musical events as the Live Aid concerts. Another outcome of this approach would be as the often stinging political critique offered by such UK programmes as Channel 4's *Bremner* and *Bird and Fortune*, as well as the satirical political programmes to emerge on US television over the course of the 1990s, exemplified by Comedy Central's *Politically Incorrect* (Jones 2005: 64).

Conclusion

In discussing the cultural public it is important that we narrow down McGuigan's 'cultural public sphere' to the sector directly concerned with mass media and extend its remit to those issues of shared concern outside of formal politics. This might appear to discount any notion of radical subversion, as the editorial processes in broadcast media rarely allow output to be truly anarchic and always employ institutional and generic framing and explanation. Yet the radical mood remains crucial to understanding the possibilities highlighted by Hartley that the cultural public might have the revolutionary potential of recasting media in civil society. There is also the role of the Internet in offering what James Slevin (2000: 181) describes as a somewhat hit or miss, but potentially creative form of 'mediated publicness'. In addition to their Web presence, of course, Mitzi Waltz (2005) and Chris Atton (2002) have discussed the tactics of protest and special interest groups in establishing alternative media platforms, and in penetrating the boundaries of mainstream media.

The suggestion of this chapter has been that any way of unscrambling or making sense of the public is a culturally and politically specific form of activity. In other words, it is a current, dominant set of beliefs and practices that encourage the division of the public in one way rather than another. For example, it is an attachment to the processes of democratic politics and a desire to understand how issues of shared concern play out in different settings that motivate the division in this book. Crucially, just as we will maintain that the validity of any division is only appreciable by referring back to the discursive forces at work, so the same is true of the different forms of publicness that manifest in various media formats and programmes. A main activity of the modern media complex is participating in the construction of distinctions in the artificially coherent public decried by Lippmann, in line with the construction of media discourses. In other words, public segmentation is fundamental to the viability of media programming. What this chapter has tried to do is to raise a number of debates around the cultural forms of media publicness, and in the chapters to come we will look at the implications of this cultural public in media practice.

Questions for discussion

- Hartley argues that contemporary public operate primarily through media.
  On that basis;
  (i)   to which media driven publics do you feel most aligned; and
  (ii) do these have any bearing on the terms and circumstances of your conduct with people around you?
- Corner asks for a public that extends and popularizes various forms of culture, whereas Bourdieu explores the notion of a public that places limits upon and judges culture. Drawing upon your own experience, which is the most realistic?

Further reading

Hartley, J. (1996) *Popular Journalism*. London: Arnold.
McGuigan, J. (2004) *Rethinking Cultural Policy*. Maidenhead: Open University Press.

6 Cultural publics and participation

Introduction

Having looked at the construction of a media public outside of the political public sphere, this chapter begins to examine the issues surrounding this broadly defined cultural public by looking at some of the ways in which non-political formations are constructed through public participation formats. It is suggested that these series of genres are part of a long term media drive towards maximizing the appearance of audience involvement, and that this has developed in a way that constructs a discourse of public as an accumulation of authentic voices and self-disclosing subjects. The chapter will critically assess the limits of participation in a selection of television talk shows, reflecting upon strategies of control against the value of public forms of emotionality. Overall, we will consider the potential role of the types of publicness deployed in public participation media in the imposition of dominant values and the maintenance of a form of public governance, illustrating a form of publicness that is simultaneously invoked as a form of authentic engagement on the one hand and as an object of normative judgement on the other.

The drive towards public participation

The notion that the viewers or listeners should feel as involved as possible in media programming has become an important consideration of production and marketing. Scannell (1996) describes the BBC's development of 'people shows' in the 1930s and 40s, which placed the words and activities of the 'ordinary listener' at their centre. More recently, digital technology has allowed a greater degree of interactivity, whether this is through the extension of choice and personalized content selection or the provision of multiple layers of information within a particular programme or station. This is in keeping the proliferation of personal communication technologies such as the mobile phone, email and especially the Internet, fostering an environment characterized by connectivity. Slevin (2000: 38) describes the construction by television producers of Web-based forums in which audience members can interact and trade views within tenable communities of consumption practice. These are forms of participation that extend beyond the relationship between media and audience, to engender a commonality between audience members.

Nevertheless, constraints of technology and production remain. For example, questions and comments sent to the BBC's *Question Time* may be incorporated within the post-production website provision, but are not available for use in the pre-recorded main programme. It is important neither to underestimate the prominence placed on the capacity of viewers and listeners to communicate with the broadcast production or with one another, nor to belittle the role of Internet fan communities. Nevertheless, a balanced assessment may be that instead of technologies such as the Internet condemning those forms of mediated publicness offered by broadcast and print media to obsolescence, longer established media platforms are using digital technologies to engender related but more immediate forms of mediated interaction.

Involving/invoking the public

In the opening chapter, we discussed the paternalistic role that media often assumes in dealing with the public, such as when presuming to represent the public interest and with the provision of public service broadcasting. Yet one of the most compelling patterns in the development of the mass media is the interest in using 'ordinary people'. There are a number of ways in which media routinely incorporate such voices, and for an insight into how this is incorporated into everyday media practice, it is instructive to look briefly at the print-based example of letters to newspapers. First, there is a commercial imperative behind these letters. Newspaper officials insist that the provision of a vibrant platform for readership voices can be instrumental in securing commercial success for a newspaper, in what Wahl-Jorgensen (2002b) describes as a 'normative–economic' marriage between public participation and economic viability. There is also a clear potential for readers' letters in offering a 'place where citizens can have their say' (Wahl-Jorgensen 2002c: 71). Yet, the volume of correspondence normally means that newspapers are required to apply stringent selection criteria. Accordingly, editorial staff have to determine whether letters relate to current events or debates, are of a desirable length, show flair in their composition, and are written in an appropriate lexical and grammatical register (Wahl-Jorgensen 2002c). So while the letters page seems to offer a mechanism of involved citizenship, the 'rules of entry' remain in the hands of the newspaper professionals (Wahl-Jorgensen 1999: 58).

What is therefore interesting are the particular forms of knowledge that emerge and are routinely attributed to the corresponding public. Buell (1975) argues that letters are rarely permitted to stand on their own terms, and instead are routinely positioned as part of an 'eccentrics or gladiators' opposition. Of the two, Wahl-Jorgensen (2002a: 189) suggests there's more mileage in the 'eccentrics' option, arguing that journalists tend to judge readers' letters within an 'idiom of insanity'; the assumption that only the most outspoken and deranged members of the public will bother to write to a newspaper, and that letters should be chosen according to how much they demonstrate these qualities. Far from looking to the letters page as a platform for their public, Wahl-Jorgensen finds that journalists perceive the letter page as an obstacle to rational and deliberative engagement, distracting from the more prescient debates that might arise from issues elsewhere in the newspaper. Even when public participation is as long established as this, its provision should be considered alongside perceptions that the overall quality of public discourse is diminished by the involvement of a self-selecting sector of the public.

Authenticity, ordinariness and broadcasting

In site of these misgivings, media has a long-standing devotion to ideas of the ordinary. This found form in early BBC radio, where discussions would often involve the voice of a 'plain man' charged with asking 'severely practical questions' on behalf of the overhearing public (Matheson, quoted in Cardiff 1986: 235). There are parallels with those professionalized forms of conduct among interviewers and newsreaders we examined in Chapter 3, only here we have the development of a form of 'professional ordinariness', where rather than on the basis of their professional expertise media personalities would be recruited on the basis of a claim to communion with the readers, viewers or listeners.

A ready complement to the performance of ordinariness in professional broadcasters is to invite participation from members of the public – as indisputable embodiments of the ordinary. Such participatory programmes commissioned by the early BBC included *In Town Tonight* (1933–60) where the presenter would go out into the streets of a given city and ask people their views on matters of the day. In a rapidly established association between ordinariness and spectacle, what was assumed to be compelling about *In Town Tonight* would be how ordinary people can say unexpected things, or have some extraordinary qualities. This is a version of ordinariness far removed from Harvey Sacks' (1984: 415) description of 'doing ordinary', and engaging in the sorts of activities we assumed most other people are likely to be doing, such as watching TV while eating a snack. While this might figure as an everyday description of behaving unremarkably, as was Sacks' intention, conventional forms of media representation demand an adequate *performance* of ordinariness, and this requires a degree of exceptionalness. Accordingly, those Cardiff (1986: 240) calls local 'personalities' predominate in representations of the public, over people who merely act in the way Sacks envisaged (unless they do so in interesting ways or to spectacular excess).

All the while, though, the claim to be ordinary is bound up with parallel assertions of authenticity and sincerity of intention and emotion. In broadcasting discourse, Minna Aslama and Mervi Pantti (2006: 168) argue, authenticity arises when the ordinary is articulated with the emotional, supposedly leading to a powerful 'revelation' of truth. In order to secure these dual claims, the production of ordinariness must be an emotionally convincing performance of 'self' rather than the transparent acting out of a role (even though Erving Goffman (1971) reminds us that the ontological distinction between the two is always unclear). According to Aslama and Pantti (2006: 170), the family of genres that fall under the rubric 'reality television' have consolidated and popularized a semiotic of authenticity, based around 'tears or other bodily signs of true feelings'. Yet, such displays of emotion have to be accompanied by an embodied restraint, and Priest (1995: 93) writes of the efforts discharged by participants in 'impression management', where clothes are carefully selected to avoid alienating their viewing public peers. All these motifs of sincere engagement thereby produce a representative form of publicness for what Mestrovic (1997) calls television's 'authenticity industry'.

The public participation talk show

In Chapter 4, we looked at talk radio and its contribution to a participatory political public, as well as the involvement of the political public in broadcast question and answer formats. Now we are going to look at one of the most prominent arenas for the integration of the cultural public into the media, that of the 'confessional talk show' (Shattuc 2001); the very format Priest (1995) was talking about when she referred to strategies of 'impression management' just above. While the genre of 'talk show' often includes celebrity interview shows such as *The Tonight Show*, here we discuss those shows that make use of the above constructions of 'ordinary people' (Livingstone and Lunt 1994: 38). There are a number of sub-genres available, mainly based around preferred subject matters ranging from social issues to the celebration of deviance and all arranged around the live presence and active contribution of those presented as members of the public. The genre's defining quality is its use of the first-hand experiences of public participants, so that their accounts form the basis for open discussion of issues ranging from personal conduct to public controversies of the day (Shattuc 2001: 84).

Jane Shattuc (2001) writes that this form of talk show began in the US with the *Phil Donahue Show* in 1967 and came to prominence in the 1980s and 1990s, especially through the *Oprah Winfrey Show* (from 1984) and the *Jerry Springer Show* (from 1991). Something of a moral panic has accompanied the rise of the format, presenting the programmes as symptoms of cultural malaise and moral depravity (Scott 1996). Academic assessment of these shows tends to see them according to the terms of the Habermasian idea of the public sphere, and an ongoing assertion of institutional, generic control over moral and political sensibility and freedom (Livingstone and Lunt 1994). In particular, Lunt and Stenner (2005: 60) suggest that critics see talk shows as exemplars of the perceived collapse of the boundaries between the cultural and political realms, such that this coming to dominance of what Habermas (1987b) calls the subjective and personalized 'lifeworld' has allowed issues of 'taste and manners' to take precedence over the circulation and assessment of political ideas.

Defenders of the format see its role as quite separate from that of the traditional public sphere. Certainly, these talk shows have all the appearance of a realm of public debate, where they are characterized by the deployment of a demonstrably 'active audience' gathered around the host or chair as 'moral authority' and arbiter of legitimate knowledge. However, thinking in particular of the *Oprah Winfrey Show* and the *Jerry Springer Show* (hereafter *Oprah* and *Springer*), Shattuc (1997, 2001) argues that these shows assume a 'confessional' role, as providers of spectacle and scandal. And more recently, Shattuc (2001: 86) writes, variants of the talk show format have exaggerated these qualities, so that audience activity has become an engineered series of practices based upon the performance of conflict, anger and ritual brawling. (We will return to these aspects of *Springer* below.) In another direction, *Oprah* in particular has come to situate the creative presence and discursive input of the audience in a position of deference to the controlling, charismatic presence of the eponymous host as the studio's 'typical American woman'. Both modes of development, as the shows' titles would suggest, are engineered around the authority of the host.

Leaving aside the political formats such as *Question Time* we examined in Chapter 3, Lunt and Stenner (2005: 62) distinguish these talk shows according to three formats. In one, the show is offered as a place for 'public discussion of issues of concern'. Such issues might range from how the law should deal with unruly children to systems of taxation. In another guise, the show provides an arena for talk and advice on the 'personal problems' of especially invited public participants. In these examples, participants are encouraged to admit to and discuss what are presented as unconventional and problematic issues, and are offered advice from the host and from the audience. A sector of *Oprah* is given over to what Lunt and Stenner call this 'therapeutic' arrangement. In its third form, the talk show acts to showcase forms of public revelation and conflict, examples of which include *Springer*. There is a considerable degree of wilful overlap between these formats, and shows that adopt the rhetoric of therapy and healing are often engineered to produce the spectacle of conflict.

Although we have so far emphasized the position and authority of the host, the various participants are just as important to understanding the format. Through the late 1980s to the early 1990s, Livingstone and Lunt (1994) conducted a number of surveys and interviews on the 'structure and reception' of talk shows, including various forms of studio participant (both lay and expert) and at-home viewers. Much of their analysis concerns the way in which the programmes operate with various forms of self. In part, these concern constructions of self as authentic and sincere; what Tolson (1991) has highlighted as the obligation to engage in the performance of 'being oneself'. Also, these performances of identity routinely involve occupying particular social roles, such as a victim of crime, a concerned parent or friend, or a rebellious teenager. How these compositions of selves are gathered as a studio public varies between shows, and while in *Donahue* the host tries to engineer moderation in his studio audience, in *Oprah* she prefers a clash of views (Livingstone and Lunt 1995: 43). However, Livingstone and Lunt (1995: 37–40) emphasize that whatever the intentions behind the production of a programme, the audience retains in some measure the power of constant and productive reinvention, and at least a part of this creative capacity concerns the realization of forms of selfhood. This is developed later by Gamson (1998), when he positions the talk show as a facilitator of otherwise marginal and aberrant formations of identity.

However, while acknowledging this creative capacity, there are a number of mechanisms of control that regulate participants and discussion in these programmes. These are necessary, Livingstone and Lunt (1995: 51) argue, to balance the production of talk against the generation of uncontrolled chatter. Their interviews suggest that participatory conduct is shaped according to an internalized perception of a fitting public persona, thereby producing a form of self-management based on perceived appropriateness for a public context. Furthermore, Livingstone and Lunt (1995: 61–4) point out, hitherto marginalized members of the audience may be integrated into a narrative of the show, with both they and the participants moving in and out of such positions as 'hero' or 'patient'. Even assuming that the narrative of a show remains stable – which will not necessarily be the case – these positions within the narrative are subject to continual shift, and the subject positions may be reappointed in accordance with the movement of the show's dialogue (Livingstone and Lunt 1995: 69). The relations of power in these programmes are therefore complex, although many of these relations are played out through performative constructions of self and the strategic use of forms of public subjectivity.

Authenticity and public judgement

In this section, we will explore how participants are accorded a place within a moralizing set of generic practices. The first extract we will look at was used by Andrew Tolson (2006) to illustrate how the performance of 'being ordinary' contributes to talk show discourse, and it also demonstrates the extent to which performance, and in particular the performance of selfhood and authenticity, can have a role in determining the course of the narrative of the show in ways that are subject to forms of public judgement. The programme under discussion is the US-based talk show *Sally Jesse Raphael,* and the extract showcases an attempt by the participant Dave to be reconciled with Beth. We join the participants after Dave has spoken and has gained the sympathy of the audience, and Beth starts to offer her account:

```
SJR:   Beth (.) you heard what Dave had to say about your marriage   1
B:     Yes I did
SJR:   Okay can we hear your side of it?
       Erm I was together with him for seventeen ye:ars
       erm he controlled every aspect of my life [I=                   5
Aud:                          [oooooh
B:                                =I couldn't I wasn't allowed to (.)
       get my hair cut I couldn't go out with any of my fri:ends
Aud:   [oooooh
D:     [that's not true                                               10
B:     Everything had to be approved by him. He did what he
```

	wanted to do. I – if we made plans it w– it was <u>his</u> plans	
	it was never (.) mine erm	
SJR:	But two years ago things must have been all right	
B:	Erm no actually they weren't. I er I love my	15
	youngest daughter tremendously I wouldn't never	
	trade her (.) but I was told by two or three different	
	doctors not to even try to get pregnant I'd some health	
	problems. He didn't erm [SJR: okay] he didn't seem	
	to care he wanted to have another kid [and	20
Aud:	[oooooh oooooh oooooh	
D:	[oh that's untrue	
SJR:	You say that Dave was abusive to you for seventeen years,	
	how did you finally, verbally abusive or physically	
	abusive or both?	25
B:	Well there was some physical violence in our	
	relationship [D: oooh] but the majority of it was mental	
	abuse	
SJR:	What did he do to you?	
B:	Erm he would call me stupid and fat and [erm=	30
Aud:	[oooooh	
D:	[Oh Beth	
B:	=and things you know if I did something (.) that he didn't	
	think was good he would just go aaah [he was always	
SJR:	[With four children how did you get – how did	35
	you get away then if this is true?	
B:	Erm the last incident occurred over a coupon he got	
	very angry because he couldn't find this coupon he	
	started taking it out on (.) at that time our son was	
	fifteen he started taking it out on him and I jumped in	40
	and erm (.) things were said and he finally told me to get	
	the hell out and take my four brats with me	
Aud:	[oooooooooooooh	
D:	[Oh no no. Noooo	
B:	You wouldn't even let me get my purse and the diaper bag	45
	bottles [Aud: oooooh] the police were called. They had to	
	let you let me in the house to get my purse so I had some ID.	
	I had twenty dollars in my wallet. He went to the	
	bank immediately following that and wiped out our bank	
	ac[co:unt]=	50
D:	[No no	
Aud:	[ooooh	
B:	=took every dime there was. Erm I had four kids	
	nowhere basically I went to my parent's house. Erm we	

```
                had to walk we had plenty of vehicles but I wasn't        55
                allowed to take one
D:      No no Beth this is not true [the facts (.) look
B:                                  [How can you say this is untr:ue?
D:      My son was destroying the house he kicked in a big
                [TV] screen knocked over a stereo                         60
B:                                            [Why? Because you
                pushed him ( ) because you told him to kick the TV
D:      No I said Beth please don't. Calm down (.) Come
                back when you're more calm that's what happened
B:      Oh that's a lie [I'm sorry. You're lying. You are lying.          65
                I am not lying.
Aud:                    [oooooh oooooh oooooh
B:      [I am not lying
D:      [How can you do this?
SJR:    Have you (.) Has he paid his child support?                       70
B:      He did pay child support for three months erm I've
                been gone since June twenty sixth (.) with four kids
                to support
SJR:    Would- is there any chance that you'll take him back?
B:      There (.) there is no chance [that I will take him back.          75
                No chance
Aud:                    [eeeeeaaaaahhhhhxxxxxxxxxxxxxxxxxxxxxx             77
```
                                                (Tolson 2006: 133–5)

In his discussion, Tolson points out that Beth is able to generate empathy and provoke a positive response from the studio audience by basing her position on the use of specific and concrete incidents. For example, when constructing an account of Dave's long term behaviour patterns, Beth claims Dave prevented her from having her hair styled or socializing with her friends (lines 7 and 8) and discusses his unreasonable response to a misplaced welfare coupon (line 37). Other familiar domestic objects are invoked in her accusation that Dave prevented her from collecting her purse and diaper bag bottles (line 45) as well as in her complaint that she and her children were refused access to the family vehicles (line 55). In this attachment to specificity, Beth's style of talk contrasts with that of her husband Dave, who offer the main part of his case using what Tolson (2006: 135) describes as 'generalisations and euphemisms', only calling upon specific examples later on (lines 59–60). Along with her use of material examples from the domestic sphere, Beth uses 'escalating sequences of argument' and snippets of narrative to present a convincing performance of someone in peril from an aberrant partner and deserving of sympathy and support. The main element behind the success of Beth's strategy is her positioning within a familiar field of acceptable domestic conduct.

Yet, Beth's position relative to social mores is problematic. A significant underlying narrative in the exchange is the pretext that Dave and Beth's marriage might be saved. Accordingly, the support for Beth hinges on her success in presenting her marriage as unsustainable, before she is able to gather support for her desire to extricate herself from the arrangement. At several points, Beth is called upon to account for her decision to remove herself from the marriage: first, after Dave has made his case for a reunion (line 3), and then when the host says she had given birth only two years before (line 14). The success of Beth's performance in responding to both of these points is underlined when the host redirects a question on the extent of Dave's commitment to his fatherly duties from Dave to Beth (line 70, 'Have you (.) Has he paid his child support?'). As Tolson points out, the dispute is about 'heterosexual relationships and dysfunctional families', and Beth's account depends in part on the consistency of her story with social class based expectations around masculine roles, to which she adds the likely incidence of domestic violence. Thus, while the extract shows the importance of a successful performance of authenticity, it is also clear that the exchange is predicated on the maintenance of clearly defined social conventions.

Spectacle and public judgement

However, just as a willingness to participate in a socially significant account of ordinariness provides one means of engaging with the talk show, another of the main characteristics of the format is its capacity to play social conventions against constructions of the abnormal (Gamson 1998). The next exchange presents us with an insight into the management of abnormality in the public participation programme. It is from a UK-based talk show called *Trisha* and concerns a woman Michelle (M) who claims to be in love with a pop star called Gareth Gates. The exchange is framed by the claim that Michelle's conduct has moved beyond that of conventional fan activity and has developed into an unhealthy obsession. Michelle's mother Kath (K) and friend Zienna (Z) are included in the discussion to corroborate the negative reading of Michelle's conduct. The extract below is the introduction from the host Trisha (T), which is designed to establish the scene for the studio audience and viewers:

T: Now we all wanna know everything about them we wanna   1
       know the parties they go to where they've been where they

shop (.) and we even want to know what they
get up to in the bedroom and with whom (.) so
why are we so into all of that and what happens   5
when it becomes an obsession too far? Well today
we meet Michelle (.) now Michelle says that she
is totally, completely and hopelessly in love (.) she's got
the whole butterflies in the tummy thing going on (.)
she's off her food (.) she thinks and dreams about this   10
guy non-stop (.) Now she was going out with someone
else but she finished with him (.) so she was free to date
this other guy (.) Now there's just one problem (.) this
guy is someone she's never met in fact she's never even
spoken to him (1) even so Michelle is convinced that   15
this is the guy she is going to marry (.) now her friends
Zienna says she's worried her friend's obsession with this
guy has become unnatural and she says she wants her
to realize she's never going to walk down the aisle with
him or be the mother of his children (.) meet   20
Zienna

(ITV 2003)

Host Trish's scripted opening makes it clear that discussion of
Michelle will draw upon wider assumptions of what is and is not sensible
conduct. The host's rhetoric moves from a mock admission of a
commonly held attachment to what P. David Marshall (1997: 51) calls
'the commodity status of the celebrity' towards an equally generalized
question of what should happen if this is taken to extremes. Following
this, a similar two part structure characterizes the introduction of
Michelle, where what appears to be a sympathetic description of
romantic love is turned to the revelation that she has not met or spoken
to the object of her affections (lines 13–15). The next extract is taken
from later in the exchange, and begins with the introduction of
Michelle's mother Kath (K) to the stage:

T: Well let's hear your mum and see what she's got to say   1
        (.) here's Kath
Aud: [applause]
K: Michelle I just want to say you've got to calm this down
        and you've got to do it today (.) ok   5
M: I'm not calming it down
T: Do you worry about your daughter?
K: I am worried yeh
T: Can you tell her why you're worried

K:	I'm worried because I just think you're over the top with everything	10
M:	Yeah but why (.) what's the big deal (.) what am I doing wrong (.) I'm not doing anything wrong I'm going to meet him and I don't care what anyone says	
K:	Yeah but don't you know that he's got thousands of fans out there	15
M:	Yeah and I'm the main one	
Aud:	[laughter]	
K:	I can't talk to her cos she won't listen to me	
T:	How long has this been going on	20
K:	Wm (.) for about three years	
T:	Three years	
K:	Well since Pop Idol	
M:	No it's only been a year	
T:	A year	25
Z:	No it's been much longer than that	
M:	Just over a year	
K:	Oh just over a year since he first came on Pop Idol	
T:	And it really is Gareth Gareth Gareth Gareth	
K:	Yeah yeah	30
T:	All the time	
K:	Yeah	
T:	You look a bit teary and a bit upset wh what's upsetting you	
M:	No it's just the way that everyone thinks I'm just off my head when I know I'm not cos I know I'm going to meet him	35
Aud:	[laughter]	
T:	How do you feel (.) do y- do you think do you think it might be a little bit scary for someone in the public eye to have someone coming on full force when you haven't even met them	40
M:	No	
T:	Ok we've got some people with hands up (.) yes what do you want to say	45
A1:	How old are your children?	
M:	Four and ten	
A1:	Isn't it usually the children that are obsessed and not the mum?	
Aud:	[clapping and cheering]	50
M:	I don't care you can say what you like	
T:	You agree with that (.) do you both agree with that	

Z: Yeah
K: Yeah
T: Ok so what do see in the future for yourself then?   55
M: Meeting Gareth (.) getting together with him and then
      becoming famous
T: Ok
M: Being a singer
T: Ok (1) so your friends are genuinely I know that they   60
      you are genuinely concerned your mum's concerned
K: Oh yeah
T: Let's not go in too deep but can I just point out
      something sometimes when something really bad
      happens to us (1) very shortly after that thing that really 65
      (.) gets you in the stomach and makes you quite scared
      about oh my God that was a bit too close for comfort (.)
      often a way of reacting to (.) you know a lot of stress and
      anxiety and fear is to get very very hooked on somebody
      who is the opposite maybe of the person who made   70
      us so frightened maybe what you're seeing in him
      are qualities of hi- his screen presence cos that's not really
      who he is (.) there's a manager saying be like this be like
      that let's work on y- on your image (.) who he is (.) there
      is not who he really is let's not get confused you don't really 75
      know who he is but he represents to you (.) something
      a safe haven (.) all I'm saying is maybe you need to deal
      with the scary thing that happened maybe three or
      four weeks before you started getting into (.) him and
      it would just restore a little bit of balance to your life cos 80
      I hear what you're saying and I think what you are loving
      in him are the qualities he appears to have (.) it means
      running away and hiding in a fantasy land when
      sometimes facing up to things that have happened are
      too (.) yucky to deal with (1) does that   85
      make sense to you?
M: Yeah (1) but I still love him
T: Ok I wish you luck ok but don't freak the guy out ok
      don't freak the guy out (.) he's only young (.) you
      don't know what happens with pushy women they   90
      frighten men away (.) yeah?
M: Yeah   92

(ITV 2003)

What is notable about Michelle's performance is the determination with which she defends her interest in Gareth Gates. This is most apparent in her assertion that 'everyone thinks I'm just off my head [a colloquial term for being insane] when I know I'm not cos I know I'm going to meet him' (lines 35–8) and even 'but I still love him' at the end of the exchange (line 87). While it is accurate to describe such talk shows as 'confessional', it is nevertheless common for the participant to maintain that the aspect of their conduct that they are called upon to discuss is perfectly proper. The confessional talk show is an arrangement that is relatively freely entered into by participants – albeit, often under misleading pretences – and the arrangement of the format assumes they will try to explain or defend their behaviour. Importantly, the abnormality that provides the basis for this show is quite different from Gamson's (1998) account of the format as a platform for the celebration of self-defined marginality and deviance. Whereas the self-defined 'freaks' of Gamson's analysis identify themselves as non-conformers seeking empowerment through self-expression, in this extract from *Trisha* Michelle tries to underplay suggestions that her behaviour may be irregular.

Towards the end of the extract, the discourse of abnormality directed at Michelle becomes more explicit, and calls upon a popular lexicon of mental disorder. While this culminates in the host's advice to Michelle not to 'freak the guy out' (line 89), the host's development of the theme begins in the form of a request for Michelle to articulate her inner thoughts on whether 'it might be a little bit scary' for the object of her obsession (lines 40). While we should be wary of overstating the correspondence between the revelatory discourse of the talk show and the apparatus of the religious confessional, the host of our extract seems to assume the authority Foucault (2004: 178) ascribes to the priest confessor, embodying a 'benevolent love' aligned with the greater public good. Beginning on line 63, Trisha embarks upon a prolonged rehearsal of what Sigmund Freud ([1931] 1977: 372), in an essay on female sexuality, describes as 'all the fixations and repressions from which we must trace the origin of the neuroses'. In other words, Michelle's conduct is established as abnormal by its representation as stemming from inner repression. Alongside the background assumptions regarding the sanctity of and appropriate conduct within the heterosexual partnership we found in *Sally Jesse Raphael* in the section above, it seems these programmes are engaged in upholding an implied discourse of normal public conduct, while at the same time selecting and diagnosing conduct as abnormal.

The possibilities and limits of the 'emotional public'

While we return to the moral underpinnings of the format later, it is worth dwelling on those arguments in favour of celebrating the interplay of emotions in the public realm. Lunt and Stenner (2005) recommend we rethink the public sphere in a way that takes account of the confessional talk show, stressing the productive capacity of 'emotional conflict' over a concentration on the circulation of rational ideas and suggestions for political action. This involves something of a break with the existing accounts of the format, such as those by Livingston and Lunt (1995) and Shattuc (1997), which remain implicitly attached to the Habermasian division between rationality (as the path to resolution) and emotion (as an inevitable obstacle). So whereas the previous criticism of this form of public participation programme has taken for granted a need to *rein in* emotion as part of a deliberative or therapeutic process, it is Lunt and Stenner's (2005: 64) argument that the format should be seen as a means of giving rein to the emotions. Hartley (1996: 156–7) describes this as a 'postmodern public sphere', that emphasizes the 'feminine' over the 'masculine' and upholds 'desire' over 'truth'. Considered in this way, Lunt and Stenner (2005: 62) argue, such shows provide for a 'democratization of culture'.

Using the influential example of the *Jerry Springer Show*, Lunt and Stenner insist expressions of emotional fractiousness are integral to the structure and management of the confessional talk show. While those critiques of the *Springer* that remain wedded to the public sphere as a political space cite the failure to manage the quarrel towards an agreed solution, this betrays a deliberate misunderstanding of the show's purpose. *Springer* is structured in order to to intensify any conflict, with what resolution there is provided by the intervention of the host in a concluding public address. This emphasis on rancour extends to the visual arrangement of the studio, where the conspicuous positioning of programme's front-stage security personnel at the sides of the stage holds out 'the opportunity for violent physical aggression in a context where the protagonists know they will not be able to hurt each other' (Lunt and Stenner 2005: 67). Overall, argue Lunt and Stenner, this provision of emotional testimony within a public realm, combined with the role of the chair as both the instigator and the summarizer of proceedings, bestow confessional talk shows with more of the qualities of a 'public enquiry' geared at airing private grievances than with a court of resolution.

Given all these differences of form and motivation, why then use the public sphere to talk about this type of public participation media? Lunt and Stenner (2005: 78) argue that the idea of a public sphere provides 'analytical devices that help us understand [*Springer*] but in the opposite direction to that intended'. It is, for example, necessary to see performances on programmes such as *Springer* as markedly 'public' in their character, executed within a space that is made exceptional by its being televised. But they also suggest a number of factors that recommend this public sphere driven by emotion over its rational–political counterpart. Whereas Chapter 2 of this book described a political public sphere under constant peril of colonization from commercial interests, *Springer* provides an effective space for 'privately motivated' discussion (Lunt and Stenner 2005: 69). In addition, *Springer* moves against the social exclusivity that bedevils the political public sphere by broadening the terms of participation, embracing 'people who are usually excluded on the grounds of looks, linguistic ability or social class position' (Lunt and Stenner 2005: 70); a development that Brunsdon (2003) describes as the 'ordinarization' of television.

In terms of their contribution to an emergent cultural politics, programmes such as *Springer* are therefore said to contribute to a more personalized form of political engagement by allowing a freely defined pursuit of 'rights, norms, public expression and deliberation'. Drawing on Habermas's (1996) criteria for meaningful public discussion, Lunt and Stenner maintain that *Springer* displays its own 'discourse ethics' by upholding values of 'meaning, sincerity, appropriateness and truthfulness'. Although the terms of the debate may be unconventional, the host and the audience nevertheless combine to hold the participants accountable to a definable system of principles (Lunt and Stenner 2005: 73). Where *Springer* makes a telling addition to our comprehension of the possibilities of the public sphere is that it adds the productive power of discord and marginality to the standard rules of rational exchange. Including the terms of the studio arrangements, Lunt and Stenner (2005: 75) argue that 'rather than being an ideal speech situation, *The Jerry Springer Show* is an ideal conflict situation'. On this account, *Springer* and similar programmes provide an alternative grammar for the expression of mediated publicness, offering emotional expression in place of deliberation.

For all this, there are important factors that undermine *Springer's* claim to be a form of emotional public sphere, many of which are conceded by Lunt and Stenner themselves. For one thing, the emphasis on televisuality makes a satisfactory exhibition of hostility the likely determinant of success in any given exchange. This emphasis is, of course, helped along by the show's own 'ironic playfulness' in setting up and playing out its debates, and escalating them into stand up brawls. Yet, the degree of spectacle depends not just on the passion with which the debate may be joined by the participants, but also on the consequence of the subject matter for those social mores, normally around such issues as sexual conduct and relational fidelity, that are supposedly under question. The thrill is in beholding in the vision of principles of everyday life being held in outrageous dispute. Since the show is predicated on the very inappropriateness of some of the subject matter, what emerges is a public court for unacceptable moral conduct. As Scott (1996: 296) puts it, 'the topics reflect conflicts over how people should behave; clashing personalities, life-styles and values; and what happens when people overstep traditional moral boundaries'.

Therefore, even where emphasis is placed on the emotion as a productive end in itself, this emotive dialogue may be seen as contributing to a regime of public regulation. First, to the extent that they offer a vent for the poignant expression of truth about oneself, public participation shows provide a public realm for confessing that one has strayed, and thereby provide a mechanism of policing the self and others. Rose (1999: 21) remarks upon how 'the management of vice and virtue' is particularly adept at enlisting a range of institutional authorities into the activities of governance. This is in addition to Foucault's (1991: 58–9) suggestion that the procedure of confession is a distinguishing feature of western culture, and his argument that 'since the middle ages at least, Western societies have established the confession as one of the main rituals we rely on for the production of truth' establishing procedures that have extended into such realms as 'justice, medicine, education, family relationships and love relations'. All of this produces a particular kind of truth, around the character, desires, motivations and deeds of the self. In Foucault's (2005: 370) assessment, the rise of confession has situated the self as an object of one's own judgement, while submitting to the judgement of others. To put it another way, confession is implicated in the governance of the self as a public person. As to the terms of this judgement, Grabe (2002) notes that while *Springer* is built on 'the violation of moral values', discussion is invariably steered towards the subjection of transgressors to a form of 'public degradation'.

Second, Aslama and Pantti (2006: 171) argue that as much as it is about the approved expression of feelings, the family of genres around reality television is concerned with 'emotional management'. This is partly manifest in the suppression or stigmatization of 'negative emotions', or, better put, those emotions represented as undeserving of public sanction. So while expressions of love, hurt and remorse offer acceptable forms of sincerity and selfhood, especially when accompanied by such visual indicators as tears, 'personally and socially destructive' emotions such as '[non-righteous] anger, jealousy, hate and rage' are more problematic. While it is in the gift of the host, allied to the construction of the narrative, to representative negative emotions as justifiable in some circumstances, such as where the woman on *Sally Jesse Raphael* is allowed to sustain her attack on her estranged husband (Tolson 2006: 134), the emotional self on display should decline physical or emotional violence towards others (Lupton 1998, in Aslama and Pantti 2006). Thus, the demand for emotional management instigates self-governance, as well as with guidance from others, according to terms agreed and acted out in a public realm.

Conclusion

It is important to acknowledge that there are different types of popular public participation talk show, guided by the mediated persona of the host and the imperatives of the production team. Rubin et al. (2003), for example, found that very different viewer responses were generated by *Springer* from those attending the long-running and popular *Oprah Winfrey Show*. This partly results from what P. David Marshall (1997: 139) describes as the constructed personality of the respective hosts. *Oprah* offers the feminized, conciliatory response to the implied divisiveness of other talk shows, whereas *Springer* viewers express an attraction to the programme's engineered conflict situations. This has implications for the perceived veracity of the two shows. *Springer* viewers are disinclined to accept the show's content at face value, while *Oprah* viewers claimed considerable emotional investment in the credibility of the show and its participants. Rather than the rituals of argument and emotional display, however, Striphas (2003) chooses to focus on the cultural possibilities offered by the participation talk show, and in particular at the contribution that *Oprah*'s promotion of books and reading gives to the development of a 'feminist cultural politics' in working class communities. In this latter perspective, Striphas' work feeds in to a broader academic discourse on the culturally enriching and empowering qualities offered by *Oprah* (see Harris and Watson 2007).

   However, one of the issues that concerned us throughout the chapter, and applies across the different types of participation talk shows in various ways, has been the extent to which public engagement in talk media may be said to be complicit in practices of governance, based upon a form of public conduct around the self. Gini Graham Scott (1996: 14–25) sees public participation media, in all its forms, as one of the sturdiest branches of an industry of the individual that came out of the consumerism of the 1950s and 1960s – a set of developments that Christopher Lasch (1979) describes within a 'culture of narcissism'. Pandering to what uses and gratifications theorists describe as the 'higher level needs' of personal well-being (Rubin 1994: 421), this drive for selfhood outwardly seeks fulfilment, but merely confects failings of individual worth. According to Scott, TV talk shows produce 'disorders' of the self in order to meet the needs of a system geared towards desire, consumption and judgement. As Frank Furedi (2004: 43) argues, the confessional talk show posits the unrestrained show of emotion and contrition as the preferred expression of the self in a way that feeds into a broader therapy industry.

Jon Dovey (2000) focuses more on the resituating of discussion over conduct associated with the private realm into publicly accessible space. That is, he points to the systemic breach of the borders of public and private that these shows entail. In this respect, Dovey (2000: 107) sees the confessional talk show as having developed hand-in-hand with a new and technologically driven culture of forced openness, with mobile telephony, in particular, casting 'personal' conversations into public places. On a day-to-day basis, this necessitates an awareness of and a capacity to maintain (or choose to cross) boundaries of publicness and privateness. Palmer (2003) suggests that this contributes to the internalization of practices of government by including the factor of public acceptability in the discussion of matters of private conduct. What we have, therefore, is the imposition of a series of practices of control over the private self into the public domain.

What this chapter has shown is that in fostering public participation, the media construct and play to readings of sincerity and authenticity. Through this, a form of public engagement emerges that presents the individual as a subject of governance. These practices of governance are internalized in the participating individuals through the exercise of confession, and is manifest as a public activity through rituals of judgement. One of the factors regarding religious confessional is the required priestly demeanour of tone, posture and measured silence that enables a satisfactory confession to be given, and constitutes the force of judgement (Foucault 2004: 180–1). We find perverse parallels in the mediated form of confessional, where the gasps and hoots of the audience provide an alternative form of punctuation, offering a full stop where the tale of yet another misdeed constitutes the sentence. What has been characterized as an 'emotional public sphere' in which the expressive is given prominence over the conventional forms of rationality emerges rather as a realm of control. In this sense, public participation media may be said to contribute to the maintenance of a form of public regulation.

Questions for discussion

- Is public participation television more usefully described as a stage for the performance and celebration of social deviance, or as a platform upon which transgressors are held up to public judgement?
- Outside of broadcast media, what formations of cultural public emerge from contexts such as online film forums, book readings and public lectures, and what differences and similarities might there be with the types of cultural public we have examined here?

Further reading

Furedi, F. (2004) *Therapy Culture.* London: Routledge.
Shattuc, J. (1997) *The Talking Cure: TV Talk Shows and Women.* London: Routledge.

7 The construction of expertise in the media

Introduction

This chapter will look at how discourses of expertise are integrated into media, and the implications of these for the construction of media publics. First, we will examine the hierarchies of knowledge that are invoked by the use of expert voices in the media. The example of lifestyle and public participation programming will be used to illustrate how expertise can be used in the invocation of forms of cultural judgement towards the exercise of cultural and political discrimination. The chapter will look at how media employs a constructed division between expert and public voices as a means of positioning the public, and of asserting legitimacy in public representation. We will then look at other, related uses of expertise as a means of exercising public judgement and contributing to a regime of moral governance.

Media and expert knowledge

In our opening chapter, we reflected upon how the very idea of public service media brings with it both an obligation of care and an assumption of expertise on the part of the media institutions. John Corner et al. (1997: 6) note that public service broadcasting, as it is practised in many European and Australasian contexts, has become aligned with the concern of the state for the well-being and orderliness of its citizens. In their simplest form, these are a series of practices that present media as arbiters of truth and wisdom, and 'position the laity only as receivers of knowledge' (Livingstone and Lunt 1994: 95). However, the different national contexts have various patterns of institutional dominance. In the case of the United States, for example, where public service is confined to smaller media producers and outlets, more representative power rests with entirely commercial media organizations such as NBC and ABC. Yet in spite of the differences, common practices of public representation run across national and economic contexts, and in public service media across the broadcasting environment. These commonalities are apparent in the presentation of programme formats and certain types of media professionals as credible and trustworthy public advocates. Whether it is explicit in the adherence to a 'public service' remit or implied in the marketing of the professional image, the media is presented as a conduit for information, but also a reservoir of insight and expertise.

In earlier chapters we have seen how the exercise of governance is bound up with the control of legitimate discourse and, in particular, who is allowed to be designator as an enunciator of truth (Foucault 1991; Rose 1999; Palmer 2003). Chapter 6, for instance, examined forms of public confession that operate within regimes of media authority. Always, much depends on the appropriateness of the speaking and acting subjects, and the division of these subjects along lines of legitimated influence. The struggle for these terms of effective governance presents, in the words of Nikolas Rose (1999: 29), 'an antagonistic field, traversed by conflicts over who can speak, according to what criteria of truth, from what places, authorized in what ways, though what media machines, utilizing what forms of rhetoric, symbolism, persuasion, sanction or seduction'. Governance is therefore partly a matter of deploying forms of media representation in the exercise of power over truth and judgement.

Importantly, however, hierarchies of dominance extend beyond the relationship between media and audience. We have seen that practices of public participation vary legitimacy to speak even among media professionals, and previous chapters have accounted for the constructed credibility of programme hosts and presenters both in political and popular programming (see Chapters 3 and 6). There is another layer of contributors to media programming to consider, distinguished from the public both in the way they are presented and in the framing of their involvement, and these are the participants positioned as experts. It is important to emphasize from the outset that even expert input is subject to arrangements of media power; aligned more with the 'traditional intellectual' as functionary than with the 'organic intellectual' as dynamic agent of social and cultural change (Gramsci 1971; Said 1994: 3).

Jürgen Habermas (1987a) offers the separation of expertise from everyday discourse as one of the defining characteristics of modernity. Livingstone and Lunt (1994: 92) summarize expertise as the discursive outcome of a rational, scientifically positivist realm that is implicitly contemptuous of what it sees as an error strewn, ill informed 'common knowledge'. This is a division that has become institutionalized, such that expert forms of knowledge have become the coinage of learned and professional organizations. Consequently, expert knowledge has also become so specialized that its legitimacy in the wider public realm is secured only by recourse to institutional authority. In parallel with this institutionalization, there are those 'popular representations' of expertise described by Anthony Giddens (1990: 89) as mixing 'respect with attitudes of hostility or fear'. All of this means that advocates of rational knowledge daring to venture into the public realm are either met with an uncritical trust or are required to deal with a self-imposed battle for legitimacy based on a purposeful lack of shared understanding. These dilemmas of representation and reception are at their most apparent, Livingstone and Lunt write, on those occasions when the outcome of expert knowledge may be outwardly counterintuitive, such as with string theory or the supposed 'effects' of violent media content. While there are echoes of C. P. Snow's (1993) celebrated account of alienated realms of understanding, Livingstone and Lunt (1994: 93) prefer to draw parallels with Max Weber's description of 'cultural modernity' as a practice of dividing knowledge into 'autonomous spheres' and institutionalizing the production and maintenance of knowledge therein.

These matters are vital because expert voices are common across media, and their integration takes many forms. For one, news and current affairs programmes routinely incorporate input from expert bodies such as institutions of medicine, research foundations and universities, and will often feature clips or interviews with spokespersons. Also, expert correspondents are routinely called upon to offer insights into a news story with relatively complex implications, such as an epidemic or financial crisis. On other occasions, there are what Daniel Boorstin (1962: 11) calls 'pseudo-events', designed for the purpose of generating media coverage, often staged around the release of a report or set of statistics and which may include both representatives of responsible institutions and those deemed professionally competent to elaborate on or counter its findings. There are also yet further occasions where expert voices will be central to the production of a media text, such as in the case of documentary or mediated lecture or essay. The particular examples that concern us now, however, are those in which expert voices are situated alongside those of the public, and where expertise is accorded a place within participatory forms of media.

Experts on the inside: the example of lifestyle television

The first realm in which we will examine the role of the media expert is their advice-giving capacity on what has come to be known as 'lifestyle television' (Brunsdon 2003; Smith 2005). This is a reality-based genre that takes as its central concern the management of personal and domestic arrangements, spanning health and appearance, household finance, house sales and purchasing, household improvements, and gardening. More often than not, the narrative of lifestyle television is constructed around the pursuit of successful transformations in purchasing behaviour, whether in the form of healthier foods or more tasteful bathroom fittings, and Lisa Taylor (2002) suggests these programmes are part of a broader 'shift from civic to consumer culture'. However, so that the possibility of disappointment or humiliation may be incorporated into the narrative (Giles 2002: 637; Brunsdon 2003: 11), consumption activities are judged as to whether they have met arbitrary standards, with results ranging from the masterful to the crushingly incompetent. The lifestyle genre presents being a member of the cultural public as an art; a set of skills in the craft of being ordinary (Bonner 2003) that stand in need of continual expert assessment.

A criticism that may be made of the form of professional media representation discussed in Chapter 3 is that it conforms too readily to the dominant images of respectable public life, in terms of class, voice and gender. In contrast, what Taylor (2002: 486) argues is significant about the representation of expertise on lifestyle programmes is its relative inclusiveness. Employed are a range of 'celebrity experts' that 'mark a new sense of openness, legitimation and tolerance towards a set of previously marginalised voices in mainstream programming' in terms of gender, age and social background. While some degree of demonstrable know-how remains necessary, such as in the case of cookery programmes, Chaney (2002) argues that any cultural shift is in favour of 'ordinariness' and approachability. Angela Smith (2005) suggests that this inclusive presentational style is designed to foster a type of expert counsel that combines easily with the performance of affability. In Smith's assessment, these experts are less concerned with the intricacies of the lifestyle concerns under discussion than with teasing out and interpreting the emotions and personalities of the 'ordinary' subjects in how they relate to their consumer lifestyle choices. In an important sense, the rationale of the genre is to legitimize emotional expression around effortful participation in consumer culture.

While, as Mary Talbot (2007: 107) points out, many lifestyle experts tend to negotiate an outwardly domineering style with displays of empathy and friendliness, their position within the lifestyle discourse is ever powerful. David Giles (2002) argues that lifestyle programmes are edited and constructed in a way that purposively 'manages' the identities and limits of expression of the participating public and places the expert at the centre of the arrangement. In an analysis focused on a UK property programme, Giles (2002: 611) outlines how judgements of taste are marked by performative displays of delight or revulsion on the part of the expert. These are also entangled with existing social prejudices, where signifiers of economic disadvantage, such as shots of industrial landscape, are presented as negative factors in purchasing decisions. While the implied social hierarchy might have outwardly unconventional elements, such as occasionally lending prestige to the taste of gay men, these only contribute to the stereotypical readings of class, gender and sexuality that underpin the format as a whole (McRobbie 2004). Within a scheme of established cultural distinction, Giles (2002: 607) insists that 'lifestyle programming is more about educating the audience in judgements of taste than [it is about] disseminating skills and knowledge' (see also Mosley 2000: 302). In this context, lifestyle experts engage in the assertion of consumption and social division over the input of those acting as the participating public, in a way that positions the public as subject to an expert discourse of a particular kind.

Experts from the outside: public participation television

While the lifestyle expert exemplifies a style of expertise based around a persona of ordinariness and authenticity, Talbot (2007: 109) picks out various other forms of media expertise. Another way in which expertise may be used is in public participation media, where expert voices are brought in from specialist or learned institutions and professions to speak with a constructed form of authority on a given issue. From the perspective of the institutions involved, often ranging from lobby organizations to universities, deciding whether to submit an expert figure for media scrutiny can be a difficult matter, not just for what they might reveal but also for how their contribution may be represented. In favour of appearing, there are the obligations often attached to public funding arrangements to disseminate research findings. There is also an ongoing business dividend in maintaining a high media profile, as well as the temptation for an individual expert to spend a few minutes in the limelight. Yet, many in expert institutions emphasize the negative aspects of media exposure. Munnichs (2004), for example, suggests that debates over risk in the sciences are better resolved through informed dispute between specialists, rather joining expert and public perspectives in debate. In the field of criminology, moreover, Buckingham (2004) cautions against practitioners assenting to the more emphatic appraisal demanded by broadcasters, which Buckingham argues have rebounded in ill conceived policy decisions. In the social sciences as well, Murdock (1994: 122) sees in the interface between expertise and the media a 'collision of professional cultures' in which the immediacy and instinctive populism of much media discourse rubs against professional practices of overview, deliberation and contingency.

However, while the pairing between the media and the expert can prove hazardous for the expert, it is a relationship that media producers are keen to persevere with. There are two main reasons for this. First, the introduction of the expert gives a certain sort of licence to the conduct of broadcasters. Marianna Patrona (2006) suggests that having an expert to hand enables presenters of discussion formats to discard any pretence of neutrality and establish their own position as enunciator of an ostensible concern for the *public* view, drawing on the opposition Habermas warns of between common sense and expert discourse. Second, media producers are in a position to set the context for expert participation. Natalie Fenton et al. (1997) suggest that experts tend to be used by the media only when a 'boffin' is required to fit with an already established agenda. It is their view that media producers are more than willing to surrender the professional integrity of participating experts in the name of pursuing emotive lines that have immediate news value (Fenton et al. 1998: 163).

To understand the extent of this division between expert and lay forms of discourse, it is useful to reflect on the terms of their involvement. The lay person, including those celebrities occasionally employed in panel discussions, is offered as a representative of the general public, but has no commitment to speak on behalf of anyone other than themselves. Even as the style is often unpolished, what emerges is an impression of unaffectedness, immediacy and authenticity. The expert, on the other hand, is obliged to speak on behalf of their discipline or profession. Since it requires recourse to authority and to the experience-based views of others, the expert position tends to be less conducive to the performance of personal sincerity than the lay contribution. Livingstone and Lunt elaborate on how the professional restrictions on the communicative style of the expert put them at a disadvantage. The expert speaker, they argue, is 'trained to develop arguments carefully, at length, citing supporting evidence, rebutting refutations and noting qualifications, they are doomed to failure in discussion programmes' (Livingstone and Lunt 1994: 130). This disadvantage is also reflected in the positioning of the experts in the studio. While their professional and institutional brief tends to be made clear throughout (Thornborrow 2001a), Murdock (1994) notes how experts tend to be seated among the audience, away from the participants on the stage and able to display none of the kinetic energy and embodied sincerity of the host.

Most of all, though, the divergent attitudes towards lay and expert speakers is apparent in the host's conduct of the programmes. In their analysis of the BBC's *Kilroy*, Livingstone and Lunt (1994: 103) note how the eponymous host's questions to expert speakers tend to be hostile and reproachful, in contrast to a generally sympathetic attitude towards lay speakers. 'Ordinary' audience members are also routinely supported in their questioning of experts, with host Robert Kilroy-Silk often joining in to accuse expert speakers of failing to answer questions. Citing Erving Goffman's (1981: 149) notion of the 'embedded speaker', Livingstone and Lunt (1994: 129) describe how Kilroy talks only on behalf of the lay members of the audience and the public at large, accepting anecdotes from lay speakers at face value and using them to begin and end programmes (Livingstone and Lunt 1994: 108). Confirming the fears expressed by Buckingham (2004), the host also sets the arguments of expert speakers against one another and, in an echo of the 'public ventriloquism' discussed by Brunsdon and Morley (1978: 8), interprets and judges the worth of expert contributions in lay terms, often reducing these accounts to nonsense in the process. In *Kilroy*, accounts given from personal experience are placed at the centre of the programme, and are supported over expert input.

In her own critique of *Kilroy*, Helen Wood (2001) sets out to provide an analysis that takes account of the imperative of such programming to provide an entertainment spectacle. What this entertainment imperative requires is not just an adherence to an established formula – such as the pitting of expert speakers against one another and against the lay experience of guests – but also the management of interaction towards particular sorts of discursive outcomes. Accordingly, in spite of the apparent spontaneity behind those expressions of lay sincerity that characterize the genre, the discursive structure of the participation show is 'rule governed' (Wood 2001: 66). These rules pit the expression of 'the lived experience of the citizen' against the 'institutional discourses of the expert' aligned with a bureaucratic 'system' (Wood 2001: 65). The management of confrontation between these realms, and with it the successful progress of the show, depends upon the host's selection and subsequent treatment of speakers, which is based on their 'prior knowledge' of the communicative intensions of each participant and their likely place in the narrative of the show. Question and answer exchanges are therefore based on 'pseudo-open questions'. They have more in common with an 'exam' form of query in which information already known to the question is requested, than they do with 'real' questions in which unknown information is sought. Throughout, any process of revelation takes place for the benefit of what Wood calls 'the overhearing audience', including both those fellow discussants in the studio and the implied public at large. Wood argues that the key role of the host is to manipulate any contributions to fit with the programme's overall theme or agenda.

The episode of *Kilroy* Wood examines is one in which the racial even-handedness of police is offered for debate, and representatives of the police authorities are included as discursive participants. Wood shows how the host manages an agenda that moves around sub-components of the main theme of systemic police misconduct, including the accusation of police racism. Speakers are selected on the basis of the host's prior knowledge of their back story, and are integrated into the discourse of the programme using what Wood (2001: 75) calls 'agenda-seeking questions'. Indeed, Wood points out that the host routinely paraphrases versions of the agenda in a distilled line – in one instance, declaring of the police 'they're racist' – temporarily switching from the role of the facilitator of an antisystem discourse to its originator. Always, in such cases, the host expresses a modality consistent with the expression of a self-evident truth rather than a highly contestable political claim. Overall, Wood (2001: 77) suggests that the host uses question and answer sequences as a means of controlling the discussion, so that the 'seemingly spontaneous discussion' is managed even to the point of misrepresenting or exaggerating lay contributions (Wood 2001: 81).

We have already mentioned the advantage the host has in being able to move around the studio, while the audience and experts remain relatively stationary. In terms of how this movement is deployed, the host displays a support for the lay participants which is in marked contrast to his attitude towards experts. This is particularly apparent in the proximity and orientation of the host's body to whoever is speaking, such that the host sits alongside lay speakers, offering supportive touches of the hand and words of encouragement. This contributes to an overall strategy in which the host helps members of the studio audience establish claims to authenticity and truth (Thornborrow 2001a).

This differs from the host's attitude towards expert speakers. In an overt display of contempt for their supposed cant and evasiveness, the host maintains a greater distance from experts, peppers their contributions with 'aggressive interruptions', and as often as not prevents expert speakers from completing their turn (Wood 2001: 82–4). Using such strategies as systematic interruptions and the escalation of emotive language (Wood gives the example of a reformulation of 'an anxious situation' to 'a scandal'), the host undermines the input of any expert speaker that seeks to present an institutional position by demanding they readdress themselves to the individual circumstances provided by any given lay participant, often restated in an embroidered form by the host themselves (Wood 2001: 84). Notably, the host allows the expert speaker to proceed unimpeded when they provide the 'desired televisual moment' by stepping outside of their institutional or professional constraints to directly contradict a personal account offered by one of the lay participants, in a way that temporarily embodies the clash between life-world and system. All in all, Wood (2001) argues that programmes such as *Kilroy* seek to present a popularized account of legitimate public discourse, torn from what are presented as the 'competing' discourses of expertise, bureaucracy and system.

Expertise and public morality

However, while the focus so far has been on media representation of expert discourses as conflicting with a loosely conceived public interest, expertise is also central to the maintenance of constructions of public morality. This role for the exercise of specialized authority is apparent in Foucault's work on institutional regimes of diagnosis and judgement. In *The Birth of the Clinic*, Foucault (1973: 120) notes how what he terms the 'medical gaze' has transcended the status of intellectual judgement to the provision of a 'concrete sensibility', an exercise in unalloyed truth answerable only to the sensory powers institutionally inscribed in the position of the medical practitioner. The authority of expert judgement applied to the body can be such that it translates to broader practices of instructed vigilance and self-surveillance over the activities and hygiene of the self. In the morality of personal conduct, then, institutional expertise can offer a potent force.

One manner in which experts are regularly used as publicly available fonts of moral authority are the consultative media genres exemplified by late night phone-in programmes, or those newspaper and magazine pages and programme segments offering media, legal or financial advice. Public participation television too, calls upon a productive form of expert discourse that develops a link between approved forms of expertise and moral assessment. The section above looked at how experts may be positioned as defendants for the misdeeds and incompetence of the system, or as apologists for professional practice against the righteous opprobrium of audience and host (Wood 2001: 67). However, where the subject matter focuses on private rather than professional activities, experts may be redeployed in a way that conforms more readily to the practices of judgement discussed in Chapter 6, such that they are coopted within the moral universe that informs media expression of acceptable public conduct.

What follows is an extract from another episode of *Kilroy*, broadcast in January 2003. The discussion concerns the issue of 'teen pregnancy', by which is meant pregnancy among girls below the age of legal consent. Those participating in this section of the discussion are the host Kilroy

(K) and two young women that have experienced teenage pregnancies, namely, Jessica (J) and an audience member (AM). These are joined by two experts: a doctor in general practice (GP) and the author of a book on the social issues behind teenage pregnancies (Auth). The extract opens at the beginning of the exchange and then re-opens at the point at which an audience member who has also experience of teenage pregnancy (AM) and the two experts (Auth, GP) are introduced to the conversation:

K:	Hello good morning. Did you know that not only do we	1
	have the highest rate of teen pregnancy in Europe, and	
	we do, have had for a long time but we now have a massive	
	rise in sexually transmitted diseases among teenagers?	
	Why are kids as young as twelve having sex? Why are	5
	they Jessica?	
J:	'Cause they want to. Some of their friends always=	
K:	=How old were you?	
J:	Did it went I was fourteen	
K:	When you were fourteen?	10
J:	Yeah	
K:	And why did you at fourteen? 'Cause it's actually illegal	
	then and underage as well. Did you know that?	
J:	'Cause=	
K:	=And you knew that? And that didn't matter?	15
J:	Not really	
K:	Ok we'll leave that to one side. So why did you?	
J:	'Cause I felt ready and wanted to=	
K:	=and was it a frequent thing that you did?	
J:	Em sort of	20
K:	And did you have more than one partner?	
J:	Yeah I've had four partners.	
K:	And how old are you now?	
J:	Sixteen	
K:	And when did you get pregnant?	25
J:	Fifteen	
	[...]	
AM:	=I went to my doctor and he shouted at me because	
	I was underage and I was scared of my mum finding out	
Auth:	Can I ask a question? Why were you scared of your mum	30
	finding out?	
AM:	Because we were having underage sex	
Auth:	Yeah but a deeper reason. Do you think your mum is out to	
	wreck your fun or is she out to get the best for you she can?	

AM:	She's probably out to get the best for me but =	35
Auth:	=and didn't you know that?	
AM:	Not at the time. At the time I'd have thought she's	
	have shouted at me because of the law not=	
GP:	=There is a medical explanation why parents advise	
	their children not to have sex and why the law, which	40
	is decided by society not outside, puts the age at sixteen.	
	And the medical explanation is this: that we are	
	growing all the time from the age of twelve to sixteen.	
	You can see suddenly between twelve and sixteen	
	children grow. The male and female organs they	45
	develop and grow to the size you will be for the rest	
	of your life and similarly the uterus, which has to carry	
	the baby, is not large enough at the age of twelve,	
	thirteen, fourteen, fifteen until sixteen is the time	
	you stop growing. And that is one reason why so that	50
	there was dancing, cinemas, all the religions had	
	sense and they preached. The damage done then you have	
	for the rest of your life	
K:	So apart from emotionally there is a good physical reason	
	physical development	55
AM:	So why then in some countries is the age younger than	
	that?	
GP:	In those countries where people marry young	
	consummation doesn't take place straight away	59

(ITV 2006)

As generic convention demands, the host (K) establishes the agenda at the beginning of the segment. This opening address sets the discussion within parameters of moral expectation and establishes the span of address. In an evocation of the link between bio-morality and sexual health an immediate link is made between teenage pregnancy and sexually transmitted disease, and the issue at stake is reformulated as a rhetorical question ('why are kids as young as twelve having sex?'). The pursuit of this public discussion of morality continues with a series of opening questions to Jessica, whether she was aware her actions were illegal (lines 12–13), the frequency of her sexual activity (line 19) and how many partners were involved (line 21). Also used through the opening lines is an inclusive 'we' ('not only do we have ... but we now have'), with the implication these problems extend beyond those on stage across the listening public (in this instance, it is certain that it is the UK public being addressed because of the context of the broadcast and the explicit comparison with a wider Europe).

It is towards the end of the segment that the two experts are introduced to the exchange, whereupon they occupy different but complimentary positions: variants of the standard roles of specialist author and health professional (Livingstone and Lunt 1994: 107), which generate what Drew and Sorjonen (1997) describe as 'institutionally specific' forms of talk. The author (Auth) pursues a line on social implications, adopting a counselling type strategy towards AM of formulating questions with a preferred answer already in mind, something that Bergmann (1992: 137) describes as the psychiatric practice of 'asking' in order to 'tell the candidate patients something about themselves'. The doctor (GP) then presents an extended account around the maintenance of health (lines 39–53), which moves from the legal context, to the accepted medical view, before extending their standard remit with some speculative remarks on the relationship between religion and social control. In comparison with the other assessments of *Kilroy*, the conduct of the host is very different here. It is noticeable that where the experts contribute to the moral agenda of the programme, they are permitted to keep the floor (that is, the right to continue speaking) for relatively extended periods. Indeed, the host's only contribution is to exercise their role as summarizer to recap the importance of the medical perspective (lines 54–55).

We should realize, then, that the constructed relationship between the expert and the public is not fixed, and depends on the circumstances of the exchange, as determined in large part by the agenda of the programme. In this extract, a matter of personal conduct posited as warranting public exposure and discussion is also presented as requiring institutional intervention. In essence, 'we' (the watching public and national public by extension) are seen to have a moral problem which calls for the exercise of expert and moral authority, and this necessitates a shift in the status of the expert from an institutional standard against which the host can assert their devotion to the cause of the ordinary public, to an arbiter of moral conduct and governance. Just as important, however, is the conditionality upon these practices of expertise that they should contribute to an approved discourse of moral behaviour.

However, it is important to acknowledge that those morally charged topics common in public participation programming, such as sexual conduct, may also come under discussion without the intervention of expert participants. This does not discourage, moreover, the use of expert discourses such as medicine within discussion, only through the figure of the host. The following extract is from an edition of UK Independent Television's *The Jeremy Kyle Show*, broadcast in December 2006. The topic of the show again concerns teenage pregnancy, and focuses on the relationship between a young mother, Natalia (N), and her former

partner, Steven (S). The opening address by the host Jeremy Kyle (JK)
performs a similar function to the extract above from *Kilroy*, where he uses
a sequence of questions to engage in a performance of mild astonishment
at what is presented as deviant sexual conduct on the part of N:

JK:	Thank you very much indeed welcome back now our	1
	next guest Natalia had a baby at just sixteen years of	
	age today Natalia wants to prove the baby is her ex's	
	and tell the full truth of their relationship to his new	
	girlfriend. Let's hear more let's welcome Natalia to the	5
	Jeremy Kyle Show. Take a seat. I know that is a big thing	
	for you today and I know that you've been quite	
	concerned about how it's gonna dovetail really let's	
	talk about you first you're seventeen	
N:	Yeah	10
JK:	Single mum	
N:	Yeah	
JK:	How old's the baby?	
N:	One	
JK:	One. Em. More than one potential father though (1)	15
N:	I don't think so it's just	
JK:	Let's talk about you and Steven that's what the story	
	centres on today.	
	Let's go back to how you met Steven and how you	
	came to be together tell us tell us everything	20
N:	I met him about three years ago then em start sleeping	
	with him about half a year after	
JK:	But you didn't use protection	
N:	No	
JK:	Why	25
N:	Coz there weren't nout there	
JK:	Sorry	
N:	There weren't nout there	
JK:	There was no reason to. So you start sleeping with this	
	guy and is he the only man I mean we have to get to the	30
	bottom of this story was he the only one you were	
	sleeping with at the time	
N:	Yeh	
JK:	And was it a relationship or was it just casual sex?	
N:	Yeah it was. It weren't a relationship	35
JK:	So what you were both free to be with other people it was	
	just erm you you said something that scared me you said	
	I sort of slept with him over the years if I'm bored	

N: Yeah

JK: I don't fancy him I don't love him I don't wanna go out   40

       with him I just want to have sex with him   41

                           (ITV 2006)

In setting out his opening sequence of questions, the host engages in a performance of hesitant spontaneity, using such fillers as 'em' (line 15) (Schiffrin 1987). These strategies continue and develop alongside the moralizing theme. Using the conversational marker 'sort of' to portray N's attitude as a spontaneous and casual disregard for convention, the host reformulates N's brusque responses, first incorporating an interpretation of N's words into his own response (lines 37–8) and then summarizing N's approach to her relationship with S (lines 40–1). Also in common with the other public participation programmes we have examined, this underlying framework of acceptable public morality operates along with discourses around sexual health and biopolitics. These are especially apparent in the following extracts from the same exchange, dealing with the practices of contraception and DNA testing.

JK: So in your mind despite ok we've talking about the not   1

       using contraception but in your mind it was you and

       Steven and the DNA and we're going to do it later today

       and bring you back on a later show. The DNA will prove

       that you and he are the parents the biological parents   5

N: Yeah

       […]

JK: Was it a relationship was it sex what come on

S: =just sex

JK: Was just sex. Well I'll do the same upon you as I did to   10

       her. Don't you know what a condom is or what

S: It was just fun it were just happened

JK: Really and it's still happening without a condom isn't it

N: Not with Natalia

       […]   15

S: I asked her I asked her to get DNA test done

JK: Today we're going to do a DNA test is it going to show

       that you're the father yes or no

S: Er I think so I think it will yeah but

JK: =And what will that mean   20

S: I mean how can be part of the baby's life without thinking

JK: Coz therein lies the problem you see coz there's this

       poor innocent thirteen month old child and there's

       you two irresponsible kids coz apparently despite the

fact that you're in a relationship with Falon right,   25
and have another child so still haven't learnt what
contraception is. Sorry but it's a fact. Every time you
have a ruck with poor old Falon you run back to
her and you think that's funny do you. Why do
you do it then   30

     (ITV 2006)

There are two strands of specialist knowledge that run through these extracts. The first concerns the use of contraception, declaiming S for failing to use a condom (line 11) and then incorporating this into a general assertion of irresponsibility (line 26-7). The second strand and more complex strand of expert discourse are the references to the DNA test offered by the programme to establish whether S is the father of N's child. DNA, or deoxyribonucleic acids, is often used in settling disputes over parentage. However, rather than using a non-specialist alternative such as 'paternity test', knowledge of this function of DNA is integrated into the host's reassurance to N ('the DNA will prove that you and he are the parents', lines 4–5), and the technical name for the test is raised again in an exchange between the host and S (lines 17–18). This temporary use by the host of an expert register is also evident in his use of 'biological parents' (line 5) in preference to those descriptions of 'natural' or 'real' parents more readily associable with a lay register. Partly, this demonstrates the incorporation of DNA testing into popular expression, such that S picks up on the host's reference to the test (line 16), but it also offers a glimpse of an institutional lexicon re-established into circumstances of non-specialist use, with no evidence of the procedures of psychological assessment and counselling associated with the professional context.

Arguably, what Jeremy Kyle embodies through this extract is the reconfiguration of specialist knowledge for the purposes of public participation programming. In the analysis of the management of expert participants in *Kilroy*, it became apparent that the contribution of experts would routinely be rephrased by the host to accord with the generic predisposition towards lay forms of knowledge. Marshall (1997: 136) writes of this relationship in the *Oprah Winfrey Show*, the expert 'serves as an essential instrument' towards the host's own resolution of the show. As Buckingham (2004) and Munnichs (2004) have argued, as a consequence of this integration of specialist knowledge into public participation television, the host tends to misrepresent such knowledge as free from complexity or contingency – a drive for simplicity than Buckingham warns is often internalized by the expert participants themselves. However, the practice we see in the *Jeremy Kyle Show*, in which the host assumes sole interpretative power over such issues as sexual health, goes beyond the marginalization and recasting of institutional knowledge to embrace both lay and expert discourses within the discursive style that dominates the genre. While the input of institutional and expert voices are regulated by the imperatives of the genre as exercised by the host, we should add that the absence of expert participants, rather than preventing the use of specialist discourses, further empowers the host to re-interpret specialist and institutional forms of knowledge.

Expertise, public and power

The relationship between the media and expertise is therefore a developing one that might have broader implications for how we see the division of knowledge. Livingstone and Lunt (1994) suggest that public participation programmes such as *The Oprah Winfrey Show* in the US and *Kilroy* in the UK usurp the relationship between experts and the public. On this matter, public participation television is in sharp disagreement with the traditional relationship between public and expert contributions as conceived in news and current affairs, where the objective expert contrasts with the emotional lay person. It also partly undermines the status element of Brunsdon and Morley's (1978: 65) observation that in popular factual programming those of 'low status' are asked about feelings, while those enjoying 'higher status' are asked about ideas. Thus, according to Livingstone and Lunt (1994: 131), public participation shows act against the received wisdom that 'the media are conservative in the sense of generating forms of knowledge that reproduce established power relations, supporting the elite and passiviz-ing the laity'. While this is commonplace outside the empowering environment of public participation television in a way that may be seen to bring specialist knowledge into disrepute, Livingstone and Lunt argue that television opens up the examination of knowledge to a wider realm. They point to Habermas's suggestion that those forms of artistic, moral and scientific knowledge hitherto guarded by 'expert' institutions might be subject to an equally valid interpretation within the experiential and widely accessible terms of the life-world. At the very least, they argue that these shows present an interface between different forms of knowledge that will prove influential in one way or another, and see the public participation programme as an opportunity to cultivate 'a different relationship between power and laity' (Livingstone and Lunt 1994: 95).

This stress on lay over expert input has implications for the status and routine deployment of systems of knowledge. As we saw with the use of DNA technology on *Jeremy Kyle*, Livingstone and Lunt (1994: 96) use examples such as psychiatry to show how expert forms of knowledge come to be used in 'everyday' discourse. So removed from its institutional context, knowledge comes to be filtered, recontextualized and, at least from the perspective of the expert institutions, misappropriated. It may therefore be said that knowledge is apt to be reshaped for the purposes of the life-world over those of the expert system, without account having been taken of the defining rules of the latter, thereby leaving any legitimation crisis between the life-world and system unresolved. Indeed, in terms of which realm has the better chance of winning through, it may be argued that the life-world offers more scope for shaping delivery to the mood of the occasion and meeting the requirements of popular broadcasting. Certainly, the discursive management of the host ensures this is the case in public participation television. In accordance with the set of oppositions offered above, the authority of the expert is therefore placed in continual doubt: 'they are contrasted with and held accountable to the laity who are themselves constructed as authentic (the real 'experts')' (Livingstone and Lunt 1994: 99).

Interviews conducted by Livingstone and Lunt (1994: 116) with a number of experts to appear on these shows demonstrate their familiarity with the difficulties of the place of the specialist within public participation genres. While it is possible to gather experience in the medium towards contributing to the matter under discussion succinctly and persuasively, experts appreciate that the discursive arrangement of the genre often militates against them. Indeed, as Fenton et al. (1998: 14) point out, experts are routinely set up to provide the opportunity of public ridicule of a perceived self-serving dilettantism among academics and boffins in general. Their participation in the public realm is often reduced to defending the use of public funds for research that the programming itself is set up to undermine. Also, everyday experience, even at its most anecdotal, is commonly presented as overriding academic expertise (Fenton et al. 1998: 127). Although this varies in accordance with the perceived education level of the audience (Fenton et al. 1998: 129), the 'common sense' described by Livingstone and Lunt is given prominence over those of the experts, and specialist testimonies are further undermined within this discursive regime by being placed in opposition with one another (Fenton et al. 1998: 30). Expertise thereby becomes another spectacle of confrontation – much like those talk show protagonists discussed in the last chapter – where the focus is more on setting specialist paradigms against one another than on making current research available to a non-expert audience. It is ironic, as Livingstone and Lunt (1994: 116) note, that the key to a successful expert performance is to reproduce all those elements of lay discourse that are considered characteristic of talk television.

The implications for the exercise of legitimacy and truth in constructing public discourse are profound. Alongside such qualified experts as doctors, psychiatrists and social and natural scientists, audience members are invited to participate and accorded a certain measure of expertise on the basis of their lived experience. Indeed, as Livingstone and Lunt (1994: 100) point out, the distribution of the right to speak between audience members and experts alike depends as much upon televisuality and a willingness to say something interesting as does on the strength of one's expert or life-world credentials.

Conclusion

By looking at the way expert and legitimated public discourses can be set against one another, this last section shows once again a complex and shifting view of the position of the media public. From Chapter 1 onwards, we have established the manufactured character of representations of public, and our analysis of *Kilroy* shows two distinct strands that emerge: one an active public with the right to be heard, and the other a relatively passive public, not in their private acts but in terms of their need for guidance in arriving at moral judgements over those acts. These emerge in tandem with the role of the expert. When accorded a position of expressive power, the position of the lay public is invested with a halo of truth and sincerity, which allows it to take precedence over expert discourse, even when the lay view is misinformed. In contrast, when under instruction the public are situated as the subjects of a regime of judgement, and the experts are positioned to help in administering this moral 'gaze', which as Foucault (1973: 121) has pointed out, may be every bit as contemptuous of reason, but is nonetheless invested with the right to shape truth.

In deciding where experts stand relative to the public, we have seen from this chapter how experts and the discourses of expertise can be placed in opposition to the interests and modes of expression of the ordinary public. This extends beyond public participation television. UK journalist and radio host Jeremy Vine commented in a programme trailer 'there is nothing more dangerous than a panel of experts' (19 May 2006). The early work of Brunsdon and Morley (1978: 7) found the media express this suspicion of expertise as getting to 'the heart of the matter' on behalf of the public and against the interests of the elite. This is predicated upon a conflict of interest between the experts and the public, based on both mode of expression and material interest, and in which the media are seen to act for the authentic public.

It is necessary to consider the interests of this media format in sustaining this opposition as a way of giving weight to their claim to represent the public. The manipulation and misappropriation of expert discourse allows the host to occupy the position of public champion and continue to fight for 'common sense' and 'plain speaking'. It is open to us to take the sincerity of this concern for the lay public at face value, but Dahlgren (1995), Wood (2001) and others argue that the difficult position of the expert of public participation programming is one strategy of ensuring the format delivers an appropriate level of media spectacle. Also, as the example of the *Jeremy Kyle Show* demonstrates, the priorities of public participation programming seem to be well served by undermining experts in their expression and use of specialist knowledge, and positioning the host as simultaneous public champion and reservoir of specialist knowledge.

Questions for discussion

- Explore the significance of any similarities and differences in the host's defence of the lay perspective over that of the expert in this chapter, as compared with the idea of the media as representative of public concern explored in Chapter 3.
- Should media respect any professional obligations claimed by experts to withhold information or decline to reformulate their input for popular consumption? Consider why some professions should choose to act in this way.

Further reading

Hartley, J. (1992) *The Politics of Pictures*. London: Routledge.
Livingstone, S. and Lunt, P. (1994) *Talk on Television*. London: Routledge.

8   Rethinking media publics

Introduction

This book has looked at the place of public across a range of broadcast media genres and in various settings. We have included ideas of public as the driving principle of media responsibility, as well as the intended recipients of media discourse. We have also considered some of those arrangements in which representatives of these publics are positioned as participants within media texts. Throughout, we have argued that various discourses embody different strategic media performances, presenting insights into constructed links between media and publics, as they are played out across various media genres and within the particular context of the democratic state. All of this has contributed to our wider concern with how much the various formations of media public are complicit in processes of governance; that is, the cultivation of practices and attitudes consistent with the orderly and conscientious population (Foucault 1991: 100). In short, we have argued that media publics are entwined with issues of freedom and control.

Media publics: a summary and rationale

From the beginning, this book has sought to draw attention to the ways in which the relationships between media and public are complicated both by the variety of media and the diversity of forms these publics take. The first chapter introduced the notion of the public as an historical problematic, the meaning of which remains contingent upon notions of civic responsibility tied in with ideas of individual expression and agency. We argued that discourses of public articulate regimes of citizenship with approved modes of conduct. The modes of control implicit within discourses of public, it was argued, operate within and through institutions such as media as well as in necessary practices of citizenship, manifest in the development of such concepts as the public interest and public service media. These contribute to broader discourses of media responsibility that establish a covenant between media and public founded on particular, historicized ideas of shared values and duties.

We also argued that just as there is a variety and dynamism in the development of media platforms and content, so the formations of media public are fragmented and dispersed. In the organization of the book, we set out to distinguish two main strands, based upon a generic division in media production between explicitly political programming and other forms, including lifestyle and entertainment. This division, we presented as necessary to meaningful discussion of the political and cultural responsibilities of media, not least because parallel hierarchies of expressive power and strategies of governance were in evidence across media formats outwardly dedicated to quite different ends.

Chapter 2 began by outlining the development of forms of media public through and around political content. The argument was that the constructed political public expressed through media was aided by the development of public opinion research, which fed into the construction of public attitudes around agenda priorities. In that chapter, we also highlighted misgivings over the colonization of the political public by the interests of the marketing industry, usurping the figure of the citizen in favour of the consumer. Chapter 3 looked at processes of representation, examining the development of media as advocate on behalf of the political public, following which Chapter 4 looked critically at the terms of public participation in mediated political discussion. Through both of these chapters, we reflected on the extent to which these constructions of political public operate within particular discursive frameworks, consistent with upholding dominant agendas and maintaining political order. Our suggestion was that even on those occasions where marginal political ideas featured as public discussion, such dialogue was maintained within a relatively controlled regime of media discourse.

From Chapter 5, we looked at formations of cultural public. In arguing for the division between political and cultural forms of public, we emphasized that cultural forms of media public are still bound up with politically charged practices of distinction and representation and dealt in issues of political import. Indeed, one set of arguments we examined was that the cultural forms of public initiate new types of politics, such that the expressive freedom accorded within the cultural public – a set of formations unrestrained by conventional political propriety – widens the scope of communal participation and discussion of matters of shared concern. In this assessment, the cultural public cultivates an emotionally sensitive and inclusive form of politics, operating in parallel with the political mainstream but less beholden to political dogma.

Whereas Chapter 5 discussed its constitution, Chapters 6 and 7 went on to explore the importance of power and representation in assessing different media discourses associated with the cultural public. Chapter 6 examined the construction of ordinariness and authenticity as markers of truth in the cultural public, in which a common spectacle is the production of sincerity and truth by means of the unburdening of the individual subject through confession. In terms of how this is manifest in broadcasting, the chapter looked at the public participation talk show, where norms of moral conduct are asserted through displays betokening emotional investment and admission. This exercise of morality was also a feature of Chapter 7's examination of institutional expertise in the discourse of public participation. We found that the legitimacy of lay performances of sincerity remained in place, but was conditional on adequate agreement with the moral underpinnings of the programme, as represented by the host. Significantly, however, where expertise is presented as the primary form of knowledge is where it supports this moral order against aberrant lay contributions.

However, without rejecting the analytical distinction between the exercise of political and moral order, it is also important to emphasize the morality intrinsic to democratic political conduct (Rose 1999: 192) as well as remaining mindful of the political interests that attend the exercise of moral order (Foucault 2000). Thus, populism in political programming is accompanied by moralizing presumptuousness, just as there are political implications that arise from the moral counsel enunciated through public participation programming. In a similar manner, strains of entertainment and lifestyle media continue to permeate the genres of politics and current affairs (Postman 1987; Franklin 1997; Cardo and Street 2007), just as genres such as talk shows can be turned to issues of policy and shared political concern (Jones 2005; Lunt and Stenner 2005).

Far from undermining the schematic division of publics, the division between political and cultural publics enables critical discussion of the issues that arise from this leakage between the two. Hitherto, it has seemed as though the most consistent aspect of media publics is the extent of the equivocation they require in discussions both of concept and policy. Just as Livingstone (2005a, b) observes that the 'public' as a perceived body of common interest has dissolved into 'audiences' of disparate and shifting interests, so the very character of the association between media and public draws upon and shifts along the discursive contexts of media production and consumption. Yet all can be subject to similar critique on their relationships with political and moral orders: questions that can be more fruitfully addressed when the generic context of a given public discourse is taken into account.

This determination of focus is all the more important since, as Brookes et al. (2004) have shown, none of these complications have prevented references to the public becoming integrated into the discourse of media themselves. This can be as explicit as the claim to broadcast or write in the 'public interest' (Feintuck and Varney 2006), or more the implicit constructions detected by Giles (2002) in 'audience participation' programming. However, as well as introducing generic difference to this environment, any critique should also explore the similarities stemming from the broader discursive context. Thus, while the facility for expressiveness and mechanisms of control differ from the political participation programme to the confessional talk show, both make different use of a similar historical composite of individual freedom mixed with mutual responsibility.

From public service to public journalism and citizen journalists

We started by highlighting the problematic and yet historically productive idea of 'public service' in media. The problems around public service broadcasting were laid bare in the opening chapter's discussion of Keane's (1991) *The Media and Democracy*. To expand on what we said there, commercial media operators answerable to a public service remit routinely claim that they discharge their duties by providing popular media content which a significant quantity of the public are interested in consuming (Eyre [1999] 2005). Keane's objection to this proposition is that it ignores the influence of 'market censorship', where a deliberate confusion of public good with audience size exercises a tyranny of exclusion over minority audiences as well as over forms of content other than entertainment. These difficulties attending the exercise of commercial imperatives in public service media are exacerbated by the lack of agreement over what is appropriate to a public service context. In news and current affairs, Franklin (1997) sees the trivialization of politics as a betrayal of public service values, while Jones (2005) emphasizes how humour can be a means of generating political interest. Franklin (1997) insists that market imperatives distort the purposes and forms of public service media, leaving them equally willing to trade in instruction, enlightenment, titillation or distraction.

Even as Franklin seeks to defend the principles of public service media, a significant lobby of commercial media interests would like to see its demise. McChesney sees a substantial proportion of the organized campaigns against public service media as motivated by these concerns of brute commerce and contrary to the interests of the democratic polity. According to McChesney (1999: 226–7), dismissal of the contemporary relevance of public service tends to make a number of assumptions. The first is that a previously 'scarce broadcasting spectrum' now has the increase in capacity offered by digital, cable and satellite technology. Whereas the state had the obligation to apportion what broadcasting frequencies were available, there is now enough bandwidth to accommodate a far wider range of broadcasters (McChesney 1999: 241). This explosion of broadcasting capacity is said to mean that we are now the beneficiaries of an 'age of plenty' in terms of content (McChesney 1999: 227). The state regulators, it is argued, no longer need to oversee diversity when the commercial producers are compelled to differentiate their own products within a crowded and varied marketplace. In other words, now the amount of content is relatively unfettered, viewer choice can decide which forms of content are required, and the natural development of market differentiation will mean that even relatively limited audiences with be catered for in some way.

It is McChesney's contention that these arguments for the culling of public service media are based on a flawed understanding of its guiding principles. Attackers routinely complain of the imposition of worthy but unwanted content on a disinterested public (Eyre [1999] 2005: 220). For McChesney (1999: 227), however, the true business of public service broadcasting has always been to provide as effective a framework as possible to 'organize media in a democratic society'. This discussion follows different lines to that over the marketability of media content, and does not share in the view that access to broadcasting capacity is an inherent right of those engaged in commercial enterprise. In McChesney's view, where market forces threaten the social cohesion fostered by the democratic arrangement, helping to exacerbate social inequality for example, public service broadcasting insulates at least some of the main channels of public information and dialogue from the excesses of commercial enterprise.

Although what we have would seem to amount to an impasse between the benign paternalism of public service and the commercial and political interests of the commercial media operator, Denis McQuail offers the informed media professional as a potential solution. For McQuail (2003: 23), the figure of the media professional is crucial to maintaining adequate standards of media performance, providing a mechanism by which individuals and institutions exercise public responsibility and stand accountable. This is a discursive figure that should embody the notion of 'commitment', and as the unyielding application of a transparent set of operating motives and values, as part of an ongoing 'dialogue of accountability' with the publics they serve (McQuail 2003: 309). What this requires, in McQuail's (2003: 325) vision, is a mixture of coordinated media training and a diverse industry base, with public funding directed at media education and small scale and local media outlets.

This idea of a relationship between media and public, based upon an adequate professionalization of media designed to generate public trust is one shared by the 'public journalism' movement in the United States. Public journalism sees the journalist as a well informed 'insider' acting on behalf of the public at large, all the while drawing upon their professional experiences to engage in ongoing public reflection on the state and progress of journalism itself (Rosen 1991). As described by Glasser and Lee (2002: 209), public journalism strives for a profession able to 'better position itself as a partner in the community', and position the public realm as, in Rosen's (1991: 274) words, 'a place for citizens to act'. What McQuail recommends is the formal codification of such aspirations, and their support through a system of central funding.

Perhaps the most prominent link between the craft of journalism and the public has been the development of the citizen–journalist, without formal training or institutional support but with the means to produce and disseminate news and comment. The rise of citizen-journalism – through privately maintained web pages and weblogs – has parallels with the egalitarian principles of public journalism, although it has been driven more by technological capacity than any explicit reframing of the relationship between the public and the means of communication. Through the Web, would-be citizen-journalists have the technical means to provide ongoing and instantaneous coverage of non-conventional news items, and whatever national and international events get their attention. Whereas Aldridge (2007: 166) emphasizes the economic burden that so many free content providers lift from established media institutions, McNair (2006) stresses what he sees as the weblog's shift away from a 'control paradigm' of assumed institutional power in the production of news.

However, Glasser and Lee (2002) also draw attention to what they see as a number of problems in the project of public journalism, which may also apply to differing extents to the lionizing of the citizen-journalist. First, while it is easy to overestimate the level of invective and unsubstantiated opinion present in weblogs (Singer 2005), both they and public journalism tend to operate with a conception of democratic engagement that emphasizes inclusiveness and the popular will over the need to engage with dominant political discourses in their own terms. Second, while this is ameliorated in weblogs by the interlinking of media content and the participation of journalists from the national level (Reese et al. 2007), both practices are geared towards a 'community-based' journalism practice rather than approaching current affairs at the level of state. This can amount to a self-imposed exclusion from the bureaucratic apparatus of political power and economic policy, including those elements that impact upon the local (Glasser and Lee 2002: 219).

Furthermore, while there is merit in looking to the professionalization of media as a means of seeing that shared interests are pursued with
integrity, it is worth considering that modes of professional conduct
invariably instigate parallel 'administrative techniques' to the suffocat-
ing procedures of state governance they may be set up to combat
(Burchell 1991: 124). Of course, part of the obligation of a profession is to
configure their rule-boundedness in a way that will meet agreed and
mutually desirable ends. Even so, the overt and dynamic fragmentation
of the media public as an object of professional responsibility produces
an ongoing struggle between freedom and control. Before professional
standards have even settled, Tanni Haas (2005) notes that prominent
weblogs have come to develop many of the same methods of filtering
and 'gate-keeping' news as such longer established news platforms as
television and radio. While few would argue against a high standard of
education and cultural sensitivity among media workers, it is nonetheless worth bearing in mind that professional codes instigate regimes
of practice that are politically constituted.

Formations of publics

In spite of the complexities in maintaining an operational definition of
public in media discourse, we have explored whether it is easier to arrive
at a normative, even if disputed, assessment on media conduct when
publics are conceived as political and cultural entities. However, Clive
Barnett (2003: 87) argues that the idea of a political public in particular is
limited by its debt to the narrative established by Habermas's (1989)
description of the public sphere. According to Barnett, arguments over
the decay or consolidation of the political public are a consequence of
the unsympathetic application of Habermas's idea of communication to
circumstances of mediation – in particular, his preference for face-to-face
activities of talk, reflection and response. What is certainly the case is
that processes of mediation have given rise to new forms of political
public, able to 'incorporate' mediated publicness into their everyday
lives, quite unlike those that frequented the bourgeois salons of the
eighteenth century (Thompson 1995: 75).

For all the problems in understanding why we are inclined to think
of media publics in particular ways, it is notable that much of Chapters 4,
6 and 7 of this book have been spent contemplating how much media is
dedicated to cultivating public engagement as performance. We have
heard arguments asserting the power of this capacity for performance
(Hartley 1996) and have explored the extent to which the terms of
interaction and citizen production are rule bound and disempowering.

Overall, those media institutions with the greatest reach and political influence continue to be those in which interactivity is monitored and edited. This continued pursuit of institutional control becomes apparent when professional journalists engage in online journalism. CBS, for example, called the production team of prominent news presenter Katie Couric to account for improper sourcing practices on her weblog, based on the established conventions of news production (Carter 2007). Although institutional power will be impeded to some extent by the inclusiveness of digital technology and the diversification of media production (McNair 2006), this book's analysis of both talk radio and public participation television shows that any conversation on how publics are integrated in media should remain attentive to the instinct of mass media to police those arguments in circulation and bring approved debates and modes of discussion to dominance.

Effective regulation of the terms of public engagement permeates the ethos of public service in media in a way that cuts across political and cultural forms. In Chapter 5 we considered the argument, inspired by Bourdieu's (1984) notion of cultural capital, that discourses around the cultural public are used to initiate hierarchies of taste and thence social division. A common argument against the ideas of public service media is that in occupying an instructive role, media internalizes such practices of division and difference. Yet Nicholas Garnham suggests that the increasing prevalence of 'the market' is chipping away at the didacticism of public service media: 'public service broadcasting and the regulatory structure that sustains it is overtly attacked as the last refuge of the elitist cultural workers, who must be forced to serve the people more adequately and efficiently by being opened up to the bracing winds of commercial competition' (Garnham 1993: 191). Garnham argues that established debates over cultural worth are reduced to an assessment of market value, the outcomes of which are decided in league with advertisers and investors. What may appear as the empowerment of both the cultural and political formations of public by casting them as 'consumers' is really the limiting of their choice on the basis of what sells.

Clearly, an important element of understanding the relationship between media and public is to appreciate the terms according to which various formations of public are judged, particularly when these are called into dispute. McNair (2000: 171) argues that much of the discord around the place of the political public is based on a 'crisis of mass representation'. This refers to a mood among the political elite that the extension of the political public sphere necessarily pulls in a majority of participants that don't have the competencies necessary for political engagement: the fear expressed by Kornhauser (1960) of a surrender to the baser impulses of a populist mass. This differs from the 'crisis of public communication' described by Blumler and Gurevitch (1995). Whereas Blumler and Gurevitch perceive the degeneration of a political culture in hock to the needs of mass communication, McNair (2000: 172) describes a reconfiguration 'caused not by the deteriorating quality of public communication but by the impact on elite and intellectual thinking of unprecedented levels of mass participation in politics'. McNair et al. (2003: 41) argue that such shifts in the tone of debate are an inevitable consequence of a desirable spread of democratic participation: that is, any alteration to the make-up of the political public invariably brings consequences for the dominant forms of political engagement.

However, while much discussion is generated by the status of the political public, the preceding chapters have pursued the idea that the various formations of media public need to be understood alongside the diverse 'local, national and transnational cultural identities and processes' of cultural politics (Armitage et al. 2005: 2). This is at once a problem and an opportunity, since the relationship between media and public generates creativity as well as reproducing discursive arrangements. McNair (2006) reflects upon the complexity of cultural formations in terms of production, consumption and description. As Barnett (2003: 101) remarks, the impression can be that media publics are 'are essentially ungovernable', not least in the capacity of individuals to move between publics by shifting from one form of programming to the next: from, for example, *The Jerry Springer Show* to *Meet the Press*.

There is, as Livingstone (2005a, b) points out, some practical correspondence between the strategies, choices and activities associated with media publics and those of audience. Different publics emerge in correspondence with different media genres, opening them to the critical vocabulary of the empowered audience, but also raising political and cultural debates around media and subjectivity. From Barnett's (2003: 102) perspective, the defining feature of broadcast media has been 'the spatial and temporal absence of subjects to one another' – that is, the material separation of publics and their submission to regimes of mediated representation. As Thompson (1995: 232) points out, this has implications for our idea of the audience member-as-self, where they must be assumed to be subject to dissolution and configuration as they switch across a disjointed array of media contexts. At the same time as emphasizing the synthetic relationship between media and audience (Scannell 1996), this very quality offers various media as 'crucial sites for the formation of new subjectivities' (Barnett 2003: 102) and, just as importantly, for the shifting of subjectivities.

It is necessary, as well, to be wary of assuming too much power on the part of the audience, given that we have seen through our previous chapters the production of public subjectivities bound up with political and cultural norms. Added to what we have said about Palmer's (2003) emphasis on the capacity of media to foster procedures and practices of governance, Barnett (2003: 204) stresses that while divided between contexts, the publicly constituted individual is 'understood to be simultaneously a subject of sovereign autonomy and a subject in need to guidance and oversight'. As Nolan (2006) points out, an attack on the funding arrangements and core philosophies of public service media need not be an assault on the centrality of publicness, although it is necessary to think about these media publics in contradictory ways. They are, on the one hand, clusters of free-born, paying consumers, with the right to pursue their desires within the sort of open media terrain that can be provided by the free market, while at the same time they occupy a subject position invested with moral direction and orderliness (Palmer 2003).

Media publics and democratic inclusion

To help us arrive at an appropriately constructive media public, with all its complexities of practice and intention, Barnett (2003: 61) calls upon Iris Marion Young's (1990) idea of the 'communicative democracy'. For Young (1990: 47), the viable democracy 'requires not the melting away of differences, but institutions that promote reproduction of and respect for group differences without oppression'. Young would rather see media as an engine of political inclusion, fostering improvement in the sorts of participation we have looked at throughout this volume. What is needed, Young argues, is a sanctioned vocabulary for expressing wishes and needs associated with and motivated by the personal, in terms appreciable as 'generalized interests'. The task of establishing an agreed lexicon of public action is demanding enough in itself, but the success of even this will be determined by the extent of 'the plurality of perspectives, speaking styles, and ways of expressing the particularity of social situations as well as the general applicability of principles' (Young 1997, in Barnett 2003: 62). The democratic potential of media can only therefore be realized by purposeful diversity in style and content.

On the other hand, the preceding chapters have described a series of communicative arrangements characterized by moral, political and cultural leverage. Mediated publicness, we have seen, restrains as much as it empowers. Barnett and Young's ideas depend on the reconciliation of the various media publics in line with the demands, practices and expectations of the assorted forms of public participation and representation examined over the course of this volume. On the sort of conceptual division of public advocated here, Barnett (2003: 66) argues that the key determinates of a public sphere based upon the 'rhetoric of personal abstraction' serve to marginalize what we have described as cultural forms of public, as well as non-traditional political groups. In public participation shows, for example, discussants are easily dismissed as emotionally invested and motivated by personal rather than shared interests. In common with the approach taken here, Barnett sets up the prospect of 'multiple publics' moving through media discourse. In this way, Barnett (2003: 67) maintains, the idea of the communicative democracy can be turned towards establishing a purposively fragmented view of the public, where the 'politics of presence' takes its place alongside the assertion of rationality, and where credence may be given to generalized issues of the self. This generates space for a series of what Warner (2002) calls counterpublics, all expressing interests and engaged in debates outside the boundaries of conventional public action.

This is said to amount to a more inclusive and accessible mediated publicness: a culture that extends the boundaries of legitimate public debate, broadening the thematic scope and loosening the restraints on contribution. In Barnett's (2003: 68) vision, media institutions should seek to provide a more supportive environment for the introduction of single-issue campaigns and the participation of hitherto marginalized groups and communicative styles, including the use of those 'visual and other non-verbal symbolic strategies' routinely dismissed from conventional political debate. This opening up of the terms of public culture has been advocated elsewhere, albeit for different ends. As well as Warner's (2002) advocacy of counterpublics, Jeffrey Jones (2005) and Lauren Feldman (2007) argue that comedy can provide for informed discussion of politics and current affairs in a way that runs against the grain of mainstream political culture – a point made by Mick Temple (2006) about entertainment-based broadcasting more generally. In Jones's (2005: 57) words, 'holding political discussions in the presence of audiences – who naturally laugh, jeer, applaud, and occasionally heckle both the hosts and guests – adds a powerful dynamic to the televised sense-making of politics' (Jones 2005: 57).

Expanding the public, expanding the political

It seems, therefore, that expanding the boundaries of media publicness means expanding our sense of the political. We have already reflected upon some difficulties in the public sphere as it is commonly understood. First, there is the unity of the dominant public sphere, implicit in the Habermasian account, as a prominent and commonly available space for approved forms of public deliberation, given a need to account for various alternative publics (Warner 2002). Second, even in those realms devoted to the foremost political issues of the day, the great majority would only have the power to deliberate and offer their view, leaving a relative few in the more desirable position of exerting some influence on the civic authority, often those in key occupations and in positions of social privilege: a distinction Nancy Fraser describes as one between 'weak and strong public spheres' (Barnett 2003: 70). What emerges is a complex dynamic of power among weak and strong publics, as 'marginal' public spheres, less obliged to authority, often find themselves better placed to develop alternative political strategies outside the parameters of state government (Barnett 2003: 70–1). Third, there is the key issue of the place of the media within a public sphere initially wedded to conditions of shared space and time. It is, Thompson (1995) argues, better to think of 'mediated deliberation' as occurring either through the interplay of media content or where media content informs subsequent discussion (Barnett 2003: 74). At least in theory, this means that effective participation in the public sphere depends as much on access to the apparatus of media as the ears of formal political power.

There are some, however, that would prefer to see the terms of debate start with the definition and revitalization of formal politics rather than with the fragmentation of the public and the conceptual innovations of media, arguing for a renewed dominance for the political public as a rational and deliberative entity. We have already looked at Franklin's (2004) position, as well as that of Scheuer (2001), that processes of mediation have hollowed out political culture, and lessened the possibilities of citizen engagement. However, Nick Couldry et al. (2007) argue for an alternative emphasis on audience members, what politics and public engagement mean to them, and their own relationship with media. Couldry et al. challenge the notion of 'mediated public connection' – defined as a taken-for-granted residual capacity among audience members for intermittent citizen-like activity – as well as disputing an assumed dearth of public trust in politics, a supposedly enfeebled civil society, and what we take to be traditional and regular media use. On media use in particular, Couldry et al. (2004: 24) examine 'the range of opportunities for people to actively engage with civic concerns' in the context of their own priorities and circumstances: something media institutions themselves have long done in surveying fragmented audiences. For some, this offers the potential to encourage political participation in the audience's own terms, whereas for others this holds out the provision of yet more cheery distraction for those audience members content with political marginalization.

For his part, Street (2005a) argues that our definition of 'the political' needs to be expanded in order to accommodate a diverse field of engagement with a number of issues of shared importance beyond the conventional expectations of an idealized contemplative voter. Couldry et al. (2007: 84) are also keen to explore a broad characterization of the political, one that extends beyond the frameworks of democratic statehood into a 'public world' that includes 'health, education and family morality, race and identity, religion, sexuality, music and film, and celebrity culture'. Consistent with its problematic status, their conception of 'public' also seeps into discussion of such 'quasi-public actions' as those forms of participation available through reality TV (Couldry et al. 2007: 70). Yet, in spite of their insistence of an inclusive notion of the political, Couldry et al. (2007: 85) advise against assuming any association between political engagement and entertainment for its own sake. As they stress, and those critics of the patterns of mediatization in politics would agree, there remains a gap between activities of talk and political action.

Defining and distinguishing publics

At this point, it will be useful to reflect upon how best to manage these various and conflicting forms of publicness, and to assess the utility of a lexicon of media publicness. This volume is itself built on a division between political and cultural forms of media public, linked by their shared definition of public conduct in the media as the expression of a form of individual agency that is represented as concerning matters of shared interest. It is, however, crucial to note that the practices of differentiation in media content and forms of public engagement are not intended to mirror those categories of judgement (Bourdieu 1984) outlined in Chapter 5. Rather, the argument has been that a conceptual division between cultural and political forms are necessary towards assessing the relationship between public participation and the public involvement in politics within a 'communicative democracy' (Young 1990; Barnett 2003). The terms of public discourse emerge within the context of production imperatives associated with and constitutive of what Butler (1994) and Crisell (1994) describe as the programme 'formats' of television and radio and across media platforms. These correspondences are not straightforward, however. Genre theory emphasizes the extent to which these distinctions remain negotiable (Neale 2001) and we have also discussed how forms of talk radio are engaged in the production of political publics, while daytime talk television has a less explicit relationship with formal politics. Overall, though, in pursuing a more inclusive form of mediated public within an expanded media environment, adherents of a communicative democracy advocate the pursuit of disparate voices with a view to empowering them to articulate the concerns of the personal with the instrumental demands of political and social policy.

While talk television and other formats associated with the cultural public have political implications, the analysis here has shown that matters of political and social significance are played out in terms different to those in the conventional political realm. Although informed by the media genres themselves, this means that the division is also a normative assessment of media performance and appropriateness. Stephen Coleman argues that the degeneration of public talk into the 'shock-jock' radio show, along with what he sees as the retreat of sustained political debate, have made it necessary that such judgements be exercised. 'Good public deliberation', Coleman (2001: 124) writes, 'amounts to more an equation between technology and civil space. People need to learn how to argue'. While these differences of approach are reflected in the packaging and presentation of the formats, the distinctions also reside in the place of the self and the emphasis on expressions of the private in the performance. It is true that, as Livingstone (2005b: 28) points out, public conduct is motivated by understandings and beliefs rooted in private experience. Yet for all that, performances of the personal as reflected in these formats rarely seek to influence the organization and politics of communal life. Even Lunt and Stenner's (2005) celebratory idea of an 'emotional public sphere' describes a space designed to reflect upon and compare varieties of private experience rather than raising actionable matters of public concern. For their part, many proponents of cultural politics see this is a laudable activity. Gamson's (1998) analysis of the celebration of the freakish self on talk television, for example, shows a diversity of voices founded on the maintenance of the division between personal conduct and public policy campaigning, perhaps with an eye to longer term institutional tolerance. Importantly, while such factors of intention and projected outcome may enter into the account, the idea of a communicative democracy demands that these different forms of media publics be assessed in their own terms.

The final assumption behind media publics that we wish to call into question is what Barrett sees as a contrived link between public activity and governmental space. In a discussion of Garnham's (1992) argument that the nation state should provide the notional space for productive discussion, Barnett (2003: 77) argues rather that the horizon of publicness should extend beyond the traditional confines of the territorial state. This vision of the public sphere, and the constitution of the political public, is as much beholden to the developing character of contemporary state power as the globalizing influence of media, as can be seen from the developing scholarship on an emergent European public sphere (Fossum and Schlesinger 2007). Yet governments at all levels operate alongside, are blocked by, and draw sustenance from cross-national networks of power, influence and interest; from international charities to software manufacturers. An increasing number of public spheres are concerned less with overseeing the effective administration of state, and more with the pursuit of transnational issues such as the protection of dispersed economic interests, the environment and migration.

Optimistically, the idea of a transnational public might even be the driving force for extending the rules of discussion and the definition of the political, including the transcendence of state power. Arguably, this is better served by the cultural public described in Chapter 5, at least to the extent that the issues under discussion forego state power and draw instead upon the expression of the private towards general principles of shared morality, albeit in ways that situate discussion within discourses of control. Assuredly, this, coupled with their relative freedom from obligations for timeliness and immediacy, is why public participation programmes lend themselves more readily to international syndication than those programmes associated with the state centred political public sphere, such as *Meet the Press* in the US and *Question Time* in the UK. While a number of specialist news channels such as CNN market themselves beyond the state level, this is on the basis that their coverage is *inter*national in character. News and comments is delivered from within clearly defined state or city parameters (van Ginneken 1998: 128–9), rather than offering a cross-national demonstration of the irrelevance of such spaces (Paterson 1998: 87).

So while the political public amounts to a normative ideal, it is more integral to some media formats than others (Wessler and Schultz 2007). Moreover, it stays contained within the default parameters of nation in a way that might insulate public discussion from emergent forms of cross-national politics. Yet, to the extent that the public sphere should provide a discursive link between the civil and governmental realms of action, it still remains that developments in the configuration of the political public should be aligned with the extending frameworks of representative government. In other words, although Barnett (2003) emphasizes the need for public discourse to look beyond the narrow interests of the legislative territory, the link between public and space has an ongoing relationship between governmental boundaries and the communicative environment.

Conclusion

Throughout this book, we have argued that the media public is a complex and fragmented entity. The very structure of the book has emphasized the divisibility of media publics between political and cultural realms. However, we have always insisted that this should not read as a claim either of a politics free of culture or of a culture free from politics. While those judgements exercised upon and within media publics remain arbitrary, all are bound up with the movement of cultural, moral and political power. Just as important as all of this, however, is the link between media publics and activities of media consumption – that is, between media genres and types of public subjectivity. As Couldry et al. (2007: 128) point out, 'public connection' is at its strongest when media consumption emerges as part of a broader complex of related public–political action. Nevertheless, analysis of the relationship between media and forms of publicness need to situate these concerns alongside discursive conventions and practices of governance associated with this generic division in and across media. It is on the basis of such a critical understanding of the range of media subjectivities available at different times and bound up with different practices of media engagement that discussion of media and their publics can be made more meaningful.

Questions for discussion

- Which nationally bounded publics warrant your affinity or obligation, and which publics that transcend geographical boundaries? What remaining factors do you think expand or contain the terms of our publicness?
- To what extent do divisions such as that between political and cultural forms of public impede the development of an inclusive 'communicative democracy'? Is there anything in media content that a meaningful conception of democratic citizenship should exclude, and if so why?

Further reading

Barnett, C. and Low, M. (eds) (2004) *Spaces of Democracy*. London: Sage.
Warner, M. (2002) *Publics and Counterpublics*. New York: Zone.

Key figures and their thoughts

Michel Foucault (1926–1984) was a social historian, theorist, and political activist, interested in the exercise and movement of power. His work tended to ally these theoretical pursuits with a concern for those marginalized or held in disgrace. Foucault's early works tried to reveal the discourses through which power is expressed as knowledge. These included an examination of the development of 'madness' as a means of defining, setting apart and silencing unacceptable conduct (1967: 81), as well as a study of the organization of knowledge in the human sciences and its attendant construction of 'man' as an object of contemplation and assessment (1970). Foucault then turned to the discharge of knowledge as power in the context of the institution. In *Discipline and Punish*, he examined the shift in the rationale of punishment from spectacle to reform, looking at the 'Panoptican' model of prison architecture – a design by Jeremy Bentham in which a central observation tower keeps all cells and inmates within sight and under possible observation. The fear that one might be under scrutiny, Foucault argues, acts to produce a surveillance driven arrangement of power 'that should tend to render its actual exercise unnecessary' (1977: 201). What emerges as the internalization of judgement was developed further in the first volume of his *History of Sexuality* series, where Foucault (1984) examined the confessional as a means of commenting upon and monitoring the conduct of the self. It is this interest in the instigation of orderliness as it may be exercised over the 'population' that drove Foucault's (1991) thinking on 'governmentality'.

Jürgen Habermas (1929–) has spent much of his life as Professor at the University of Frankfurt. He emerged from and has been influenced by the 'Frankfurt School' of critical theory, having worked with Theodor W. Adorno in the 1950s. Habermas's vast works include an interest in developing a systematic means of offsetting the colonization of legitimate public discourse by intuitive and folk knowledge (1985: 8), while at the same time constructing a 'universal pragmatics' for assessing and improving the communicative environment within which political debates are played out (1984; 1987b). His work on 'the public sphere' has provided a dominant means for conceptualizing the relationship between media and politics, and a useful analogy for describing the virtual space within which media's contribution to political discussion ordinarily functions. While he continues to assert the importance of the public sphere, Habermas's recent work has been on the development of the European Union as a democratic space.

Walter Lippmann (1889–1974) was both a major figure in journalism and an adviser to US political figures including President Franklin D. Roosevelt. As a journalist and editor, Lippmann worked for the *New York World* and went on to produce a regular column for the *Herald Tribune*. In 1962, he was also awarded the Pulitzer Prize for International Reporting. *Public Opinion* (1922) is Lippmann's third book of ten, and has emerged as the most influential. In it, he argued that the political establishment maintain a conceit of the public as well informed and competent, when there is no reason to suppose that the average member of the public has the inclination or the means to be either of these. The consequence of this has been that both the political and the media establishments abdicate their decision-making role in favour of submission to an amorphous popular will – inventing coherence where none is possible. In *The Phantom Public* ([1927] 1993), Lippmann expressed his own wish to place an emphasis on experts and intellectual leaders. This latter suggestion in particular was to be disputed by John Dewey (1929) in *The Public and its Problems*.

References

Abts, K. and Rummens, S. (2007) Populism versus democracy, *Political Studies*, 55: 405–24.

Adorno, T. W. (1957) Television and the patterns of mass culture, in B. Rosenberg and D. Manning White (eds), *Mass Culture*. Glencoe: Free Press.

Adorno, T. and Horkheimer, M. ([1944] 1979) *Dialectic of Enlightenment*. London: Verso.

Aldridge, M. (2007) *Understanding the Local Media*. Maidenhead: Open University Press.

Ali, T. (2002) *The Clash of Fundamentalisms*. London: Verso.

Allan, S. (1999) *News culture*. Buckingham: Open University Press.

Althusser, L. (1971) *Lenin and Philosophy and Other Essays*. London: New Left Books.

Anderson, B. (1991) *Imagined Communities*, revised edn. London: Verso.

Anderson, L. (1999) Audience participation and the representation of the political process in two British talk shows, in L. Haarman (ed.), *Talk About Shows*. Bolognia: CLUEB.

Ang, I. (1991) *Desperately Seeking the Audience*. London: Routledge.

Arblaster, A. (1987) *Democracy*. Milton Keynes: Open University Press.

Armitage, J., Bishop, R. and Kellner, D. (2005) Introducing *Cultural Politics*, *Cultural Politics*, 1(1): 1–4.

Arnold, M. (1863) The bishop and the philosopher, *Macmillan's Magazine*, 7 (Jan.): 241–56.

Arnold, M. ([1869] 1933) *Culture and Anarchy*. Cambridge: Cambridge University Press.

Aslama, M. and Pantti, M. (2006) Talking alone: reality TV, emotions and authenticity, *European Journal of Cultural Studies*, 9: 167–84.

Atifi, H. and Marcoccia, M. (2006) Television genre as an object of negotiation: a semio-pragmatic analysis of French political 'television forum', *Journal of Pragmatics*, 38: 250–68.

Atkinson, M. (1984) *Our Masters' Voices*. London: Routledge.

Atton, C. (2002) *Alternative Media*. London: Sage.

Auerbach, E. (1973) The emergence of a literary public in western Europe, in E. Burns and T. Burns (eds), *Sociology of Literature and Drama*. Harmondsworth: Penguin.

Austin, J. L. (1962) *How to do Things with Words.* Oxford: Clarendon.

Bagdikian, B. H. (1985) The US media: supermarket or assembly line? *Journal of Communication,* 35: 97–109.

Bailey, M. (2007) Rethinking public service broadcasting: the historical limits to publicness, in R. Butsch (ed.), *Media and Public Spheres.* Basingstoke: Palgrave Macmillan.

Bakhtin, M. M. (1981) *The Dialogic Imagination.* Austin: Texas University Press.

Bakhtin, M. M. (1984) *Rabelais and His World.* Bloomington: Indiana University Press.

Barker, C. (2003) *Cultural Studies: Theory and Practice,* 2nd edn. London: Sage.

Barnett, C. (2003) *Culture and Democracy.* Edinburgh: Edinburgh University Press.

Barnett, C. (2004) Media, democracy and representation: disembodying the public, in C. Barnett and M. Low (eds), *Spaces of Democracy.* London: Sage.

Barnouw, E. (1975) *Tube of Plenty.* New York: Oxford University Press.

Barrett, G. (ed.) (2004) *The Oxford Dictionary of American Political Slang.* New York: Oxford University Press.

Barthes, R. (1972) *Mythologies.* New York: Hill and Wang.

Baudrillard, J. (1988) *Selected Writings.* Cambridge: Polity.

Baum, M. A. (2005) Talking the vote: why presidential candidates hit the talk show circuit, *American Journal of Political Science,* 49: 213–34.

BBC (2006) Transcript, *Any Questions?* 20 Jan. Available at: www.bbc.co.uk/radio4/news/anyquestions_transcripts_20060120.shtml

Bennett, T., Grossberg, L. and Morris, M. (eds) (2005) *New Keywords.* Oxford: Blackwell.

Berelson, B. and Janowitz, M. (1966) *Reader in Public Opinion and Communication,* 2nd edn. New York: Free Press.

Bergmann, J. R. (1992) Veiled morality: notes on discretion in psychiatry, in P. Drew and J. Heritage (eds), *Talk at Work.* Cambridge: Cambridge University Press.

Blumler, J. G. (2001) The third age of political communication, *Journal of Public Affairs,* 1: 201–9.

Blumler, J. G. and Gurevitch, M. (1995) *The Crisis of Public Communication.* London: Routledge.

Blumler, J. G. and Hoffmann-Riem, W. (1992) Towards renewed accountability in broadcasting, in J. G. Blumler (ed.), *Television and the Public Interest.* London: Sage.

Bondebjerg, I. (1996) Public discourse / private fascination: hybridization in 'true-life-story' genres. *Media, Culture & Society,* 18: 27–45.

Bonner, F. (2003) *Ordinary Television: Analysing Popular TV.* London: Sage.

Boorstin, D. J. (1962) *The Image, Or What Happened to the American Dream*. New York: Atheneum.

Bourdieu, P. (1979) Public opinion does not exist, in A. Mattelart and S. Siegelaub (eds), *Communication and Class Struggle 1: Capitalism, Imperialism*. New York: International General.

Bourdieu, P. (1984) *Distinction: A Social Critique of the Judgement of Taste*. London: Routledge.

Bourdieu, P. (1992) *Language and Symbolic Power*. Cambridge: Polity.

Bourdieu, P. (1996) *The Rules of Art*. Cambridge: Polity.

Bourdieu, P. (1998) *On Television and Journalism*. London: Pluto.

Braudy, L. (1997) *The Frenzy of Renown: Fame and its History*. New York: Vintage.

Briggs, A. (1995) *The History of Broadcasting in the United Kingdom: Volume V. Competition, 1955–1974*. Oxford: Oxford University Press.

Brighton, P. and Foy, D. (2007) *News Values*. London: Sage.

Brookes, R., Lewis, J. and Wahl-Jorgensen, K. (2004) The media representation of public opinion: British television news coverage of the 2001 general election, *Media, Culture & Society*, 26: 63–80.

Brunsdon, C. (2003) Lifestyling Britain: the 8–9 slot on British television, *International Journal of Cultural Studies*, 6: 5–23.

Brunsdon, C. and Morley, D. (1978) *Everyday Television: Nationwide*. London: BFI.

Bryce, J. ([1900] 1966) The nature of public opinion, in B. Berelson and M. Janowitz (eds), *Reader in Public Opinion and Communication*, 2nd edn. New York Free Press.

Buckingham, J. I. (2004) 'Newsmaking' criminology or 'infotainment' criminology? *Australian and New Zealand Journal of Criminology*, 37: 253–75.

Budd, M. (1996) *Values of Art: Pictures, Poetry and Music*. Harmondsworth: Penguin.

Buell, E. H. (1975) Eccentrics or gladiators? People who write about politics in letters-to-the-editor, *Social Science Quarterly*, 56(3): 440–9.

Bullock, A. and Trombley, S. (eds) *The New Fontana Dictionary of Modern Thought*. London: Fontana.

Burchell, G. (1991) Peculiar interests: civil society and governing 'the system on natural liberty', in G. Burchell, C. Gordon and P. Miller (eds), *The Foucault Effect: Studies in Governmentality*. Chicago: Chicago University Press.

Burns, T. (1977) The organization of public opinion, in J. Curran, M. Gurevitch and J. Woollacott (eds), *Mass Media and Society*. London: Edward Arnold.

Butler, J. G. (1994) *Television: Critical Methods and Applications*. Belmont: Wadsworth.

Calhoun, C. (2005) Public, in T. Bennett, L. Grossberg and M. Morris (eds), *New Keywords*. Oxford: Blackwell.

Cameron, D. (1992) *Feminism and Linguistic Theory*, 2nd edn. London: Macmillan.

Canovan, M. (1981) *Populism*. London: Junction.

Canovan, M. (2002) Taking politics to the people: populism as the ideology of democracy, in Y. Mény and Y. Surel (eds), *Democracies and the Populist Challenge*. New York: Basic Books.

Cardiff, D. (1986) The serious and the popular: aspects of the evolution of style in the radio talk 1928–1939, in R. Collins, J. Curran, N. Garnham et al. (eds), *Media, Culture & Society: A Critical Reader*. London: Sage.

Cardo, V. and Street, J. (2007) *Vote For Me*: playing at politics, in K. Riegert (ed.), *Politicotainment: Television's Take on the Real*. New York: Peter Lang.

Carey, J. W. (1989) *Culture as Communication: Essays on Media and Society*. Boston: Unwin Hyman.

Carlyle, T. (1840) *On Heroes, Hero-Worship and the Heroic in History*. London: Chapman and Hall.

Carpignano, P., Andersen, P., Aronowitz, S. and Difazio, W. (1990) Chatter in the age of electronic reproduction: talk television and the 'public mind', *Communication Research*, 19: 109–29.

Carter, B. (2007) After Couric incident, CBS to scrutinize its web content, *New York Times*, 12 April.

Chadwick, R. F. (ed.) (1994) *Ethics and the Professions*. Aldershot: Ashgate.

Chaney, D. (2002) *Cultural Change and Everyday Life*. Basingstoke: Palgrave.

Clayman, S. E. (2002) Tribune of the people: maintaining the legitimacy of aggressive journalism, *Media, Culture & Society*, 24: 197–216.

Clayman, S. and Heritage, J. (2002) *The News Interview*. Cambridge: Cambridge University Press.

Cockerell, M. (1989) *Live from Number 10: The Inside Story of Prime Ministers and Television*. London: Faber and Faber.

Cohen, B. C. (1963) *The Press and Foreign Policy*. Princeton: Princeton University Press.

Coleman, S. (2001) The transformation of citizenship, in B. Axford and R. Huggins (eds), *New Media and Politics*. London: Sage.

Connell, R. W. (1995) *Masculinities*. Cambridge: Polity.

Cook, J. (2000) Dangerously radioactive: the plural vocalities of radio talk, in A. Lee and C. Poynton (eds), *Culture and Text*. St Leonard's, New South Wales: Allen and Unwin.

Corner, J. (1998) *Studying Media: Problems of Theory and Method*. Edinburgh: Edinburgh University Press.

Corner, J. (2001) The 'public', the 'popular' and media studies, in G. Philo and D. Miller (eds), *Market Killing*. Harlow: Longman.

Corner, J. (2003) Mediated persona and political culture, in J. Corner and D. Pels (eds), *Media and the Restyling of Politics*. London: Sage.

Corner, J., Schlesinger, P. and Silverstone, R. (1997) Editors' introduction, in J. Corner, P. Schlesinger and R. Silverstone (eds), *International Media Research: A Critical Survey*. London: Routledge.

Corporation for Public Broadcasting (undated) Public Broadcasting Act of 1967, as amended. Available at: www.cpb.org/aboutpb/act/text.html

Corporation for Public Broadcasting (2004) Goals and objectives. Available at: www.cpb.org/aboutcpb/goals/goalsandobjectives/goalsandobjectives_full.html

Corporation for Public Broadcasting (2005) CFP's commitment to objectivity and balance. Available at: www.cpb.org/aboutcpb/goals/objectivity/

Couldry, N. (2000) *Inside Culture*. London: Sage.

Couldry, N., Livingstone, S. and Markham, T. (2007) *Media Consumption and Public Engagement*. Basingstoke: Palgrave Macmillan.

Crissell, A. (1994) *Understanding Radio*. London: Routledge.

Croteau, D. and Hoynes, W. (1994) *By Invitation Only: How the Media Limit Political Debate*. Maine: Common Courage.

Crystal, D. (1997) *A Dictionary of Linguistics and Phonetics*, 4th edn. Oxford: Blackwell.

Curran, J. and Seaton, J. (1997) *Power without Responsibility: The Press and Broadcasting in Britain*, 5th edn. London: Routledge.

Dahlberg, L. (2006) On the open and closed space of public discourse, *Nordicom Review*, 2: 35–52.

Dahlgren, P. (1995) *Television and the Public Sphere*. London: Sage.

Dahlgren, P. and Olsson, T. (2007) From public sphere to civic culture: young citizens' Internet use, in R. Butsch (ed.), *Media and Public Spheres*. Basingstoke: Palgrave Macmillan.

Davis, A. (2002) *Public Relations Democracy: Politics, Public Relations and the Mass Media in Britain*. Manchester: Manchester University Press.

Day, R. (1989) *Grand Inquisitor: Memoirs*. London: Weidenfeld and Nicolson.

Day, R. (1993) *But With Respect . . .: Memorable Interviews with Statesmen and Parliamentarians*. London: Weidenfeld and Nicholson.

Day, G. (2007) So much more than mere talk, *Times Higher Education Supplement*, 3 Aug.

Debray, R. (1983) *Critique of Political Reason*. London: New Left Books.

de Tocqueville, A.([1840] 1968) *Democracy in America*. Glasgow: Collins.

Dewey, J. (1929) *The Public and its Problems*. London: Allen Unwin.

Dixon, K. and Spree, S. (2003) Deploying identity for democratic ends on

Jan Publiek – a Flemish television talk show, *European Journal of Women's Studies* 10: 409–22.

Dovey, J. (2000) *Freakshow: First Person Media and Factual Television*. London: Pluto.

Downey, J. (2006) The media industries: do ownership, size and internationalisation matter? in D. Hesmondhalgh (ed.), *Media Production*. Maidenhead: Open University Press.

Drake, P. and Higgins, M. (2006) I'm a celebrity, get me into politics: the political celebrity and the celebrity politician, in S. Holmes and S. Redmond (eds), *Framing Celebrity*. London: Routledge.

Drew, P. and Sorjonen, M. L. (1997) Institutional dialogue, in T. A. van Dijk (ed.), *Discourse as Social Interaction*. London: Sage.

Dyson, K. (1996) Revisiting *Culture and Anarchy*: media studies, the cultural industries and the issue of quality, in K. Dyson and W. Homolka (eds), *Culture First*. London: Cassell.

Elster, J. (1998a) Deliberation and constitution making, in J. Elster and A. Przeworski (eds), *Deliberative Democracy*. Cambridge: Cambridge University Press.

Elster, J. (1998b) Introduction: deliberative democracy, in J. Elster and A. Przeworski (eds), *Deliberative Democracy*. Cambridge: Cambridge University Press.

Engels, F. ([1884] 1942) *The Origin of the Family, Private Property and the State*. London: Lawrence and Wishart.

Entman, R. M. (1989) *Democracy Without Citizens*. Oxford: Oxford University Press.

Eyre, R. ([1999] 2005) Public-interest broadcasting: a new approach, in B. Franklin (ed.), *Television Policy: The MacTaggart Lectures*. Edinburgh: Edinburgh University Press.

Fairclough, N. (1995) *Media Discourse*. London: Arnold.

Fairclough, N. (2001) *Language and Power*, 2nd edn. London: Longman.

Fairclough, N. and Wodak, R. (1997) Critical discourse analysis, in T. A. van Dijk (ed.), *Discourse as Social Interaction*. London: Sage.

Feintuck, M. and Varney, M. (2006) *Media Regulation, Public Interest and the Law*, 2nd edn. Edinburgh: Edinburgh University Press.

Feldman, L. (2007) The news about comedy: young audiences, *The Daily Show*, and evolving notions of journalism, *Journalism*, 8(4): 406–27.

Fenton, N., Bryman, A., Deacon, D. and Birmingham, P. (1997) 'Sod off and find us a boffin': journalists and the social science conference, *The Sociological Review*, 45: 1–23.

Fenton, N., Bryman, A., Deacon, D. and Birmingham, P. (1998) *Mediating Social Science*. London: Sage.

Fetzer, A. (2002) 'Put bluntly, you have something of a credibility problem': sincerity and credibility in political interviews, in P.

Chilton and C. Schäffner (eds), *Politics as Text and Talk*. Amsterdam and Philadelphia: John Benjamins.

Fishkin, J. S. (1997) *The Voice of the People: Public Opinion and Democracy*. New Haven: Yale University Press.

Fiske, J. and Hartley, J. (1978) *Reading Television*. London: Routledge.

Fossum, J. E. and Schlesinger, P. (eds) (2007) *The European Union and the Public Sphere: A Communicative Space in the Making?* Abingdon: Routledge.

Foucault, M. (1967) *Madness and Civilization*. London: Routledge.

Foucault, M. (1970) *The Order of Things*. London: Routledge.

Foucault, M. (1972) *The Archaeology of Knowledge*. London: Routledge.

Foucault, M. (1973) *The Birth of the Clinic*. New York: Vintage.

Foucault, M. (1977) *Discipline and Punish*. Harmondsworth: Penguin.

Foucault, M. (1980) *Power/Knowledge*. Hemel Hempstead: Harvester Wheatsheaf.

Foucault, M. (1983) The subject and power, in H. L. Dreyfus and P. Rabinow (eds), *Michel Foucault: Beyond Structuralism and Hermeneutics*, 2nd edn. Chicago: Chicago University Press.

Foucault, M. (1984) *The History of Sexuality, Volume 1: An Introduction*. Harmondsworth: Peregrine.

Foucault, M. (1990) *The Use of Pleasure: The History of Sexuality, Volume 2*. New York: Vintage.

Foucault, M. (1991) Governmentality, in G. Burchell, C. Gordon and P. Miller (eds), *The Foucault Effect: Studies in Governmentality*. Chicago: Chicago University Press.

Foucault, M. (2000) *Ethics: Essential Works of Foucault 1954–1984, Volume 1*. Harmondsworth: Penguin.

Foucault, M. (2004) *Abnormal*. New York: Picador.

Foucault, M. (2005) *The Hermeneutics of the Subject*. New York: Picador.

Franklin, B. (1997) *Newszak and News Media*. London: Arnold.

Franklin, B. (2004) *Packaging Politics*, 2nd edn. London: Arnold.

Freud, S. ([1931] 1977) Female sexuality, *On Sexuality*. Harmondsworth: Penguin.

Frith, S. ([1991] 2006) The good, the bad, and the indifferent: defending popular culture from the populists, in J. Storey (ed.), *Cultural Theory and Popular Culture: A Reader*, 3rd edn. Harlow: Pearson/Prentice Hall.

Fukayama, F. (1992) *The End of History and the Last Man*. Harmondsworth: Penguin.

Furedi, F. (2004) *Therapy Culture*. London: Routledge.

Gallup, G. H. R. (1940) *The Pulse of Democracy: The Public Opinion Poll and How it Works*. New York: Simon and Schuster.

Gamson, J. (1998) *Freaks Talk Back: Tabloid Shows and Sexual Nonconformity*. Chicago: Chicago University Press.

Garnham, N. (1992) The media and the public sphere, in C. Calhoun (ed.), *Habermas and the Public Sphere.* Cambridge, MA: MIT Press.

Garnham, N. (1993) The cultural arbitrary and television, in C. Calhoun, E. LiPuma and M. Postone (eds), *Bourdieu: Critical Perspectives.* Cambridge: Polity.

Garnham, N. and Williams, R. (1986) Pierre Bourdieu and the sociology of culture: an Introduction, in R. Collins, J. Curran, N. Garnham et al. (eds), *Media, Culture & Society: A Critical Reader.* London: Sage.

Giddens, A. (1990) *The Consequences of Modernity.* Stanford: Stanford University Press.

Giddens, A. (1991) *Modernity and Self Identity.* Cambridge: Polity.

Giles, D. C. (2002) Keeping the public in their place: audience participation in lifestyle television programming, *Discourse & Society*, 13: 603–28.

Gilroy, P. (2000) *Against Race: Imagining Political Culture Beyond the Color Line.* Cambridge, MA: Belknap/Harvard.

Glasser, T. L. and Lee, F. L. F. (2002) Repositioning the newsroom: the American experience with 'public journalism', in R. Kuhn and E. Neveu (eds), *Political Journalism: New Challenges, New Practices.* London: Routledge.

Glynn, C. J., Herbst, S., O'Keefe, G. J., Shapiro, R. Y. and Lindeman, M. (2004) *Public Opinion*, 2nd edn. Boulder, CO: Westview.

Goffman, E. (1971) *The Presentation of the Self in Everyday Life.* Harmondsworth: Penguin.

Goffman, E. (1981) *Forms of Talk.* Philadelphia: Pennsylvania University Press.

Goffman, E. (1986) *Frame Analysis.* Boston: Northeastern University Press.

Goldberg, D. T. (1999) Call and response: sports, talk radio, and the death of democracy, in D. Slayden and R. K. Willock (eds), *Soundbite Culture.* Thousand Oaks, CA: Sage.

Golding, P. and Murdock, G. (1996) Culture, communications and political economy, in J. Curran and M. Gurevitch (eds), *Mass Media and Society*, 2nd edn. London: Arnold.

Gordon, C. (1991) Government rationality: an introduction, in G. Burchell, C. Gordon and P. Miller (eds), *The Foucault Effect: Studies in Governmentality.* Chicago: Chicago University Press.

Grabe, M. E. (2002) Maintaining the moral order: a functional analysis of *The Jerry Springer Show, Critical Studies in Media Communication*, 19: 311–28.

Gramsci, A. (1971) *Selections from Prison Notebooks.* London: Lawrence and Wishart.

Gramsci, A. (1988) *Selections from Cultural Writings.* London: Lawrence and Wishart.

Gramsci, A. (1995) *Further Selections from the Prison Notebooks*. Minneapolis: Minnesota University Press.

Haas, T. (2005) From 'public journalism' to the 'public's journalism: rhetoric and reality in the discourse on weblogs, *Journalism Studies*, 6: 387–96.

Habermas, J. (1976) *Legitimation Crisis*. London: Heinemann.

Habermas, J. (1979) The public sphere, in A. Mattelart and S. Siegelaub (eds), *Communication and Class Struggle: Capitalism, Imperialism*. New York: International General.

Habermas, J. (1984) *The Theory of Communicative Action, Volume 1: Reason and the Rationalization of Society*. Cambridge: Polity.

Habermas, J. (1985) Modernity – an incomplete project, in H. Foster (ed.), *Postmodern Culture*. London: Pluto.

Habermas, J. (1987a) *The Philosophical Discourse of Modernity*. Cambridge: Polity.

Habermas, J. (1987b) *The Theory of Communicative Action, Volume 2: Lifeworld and System: A Critique of Functionalist Reason*. Cambridge: Polity.

Habermas, J. (1989) *The Structural Transformation of the Public Sphere*. Cambridge: Polity.

Habermas, J. (1992) Further reflections on the public sphere, in C. Calhoun (ed.), *Habermas and the Public Sphere*. Cambridge, MA: MIT Press.

Habermas, J. (1996) *Between Facts and Norms: Contributions to a Discourse Theory of Law and Democracy*. Cambridge: Polity.

Habermas, J. (2004) Public space and political public sphere – the biographical roots of two motifs in my thought, Kyoto Memorial Lecture, Kyoto, 11 Nov.

Hall, S. (1981) Notes on deconstructing 'the popular', in R. Samuel (ed.) *People's History and Socialist Theory*. London: Routledge and Kegan Paul.

Hall, A. and Cappella, J. N. (2002) The impact of political talk radio exposure on attributions about the outcome of the 1996 US Presidential Election, *Journal of Communication*, 52: 332–50.

Hall, S., Critcher, C., Jefferson, T., Clarke, J. and Roberts, B. (1978) *Policing the Crisis*. London: Macmillan.

Hallin, D. C. (1994) *We Keep America on Top of the World*. London: Routledge.

Hannay, A. (2005) *On the Public*. Abingdon: Routledge.

Harris, S. (1991) Evasive action: how politicians respond to question in political interviews, in P. Scannell (ed.), *Broadcast Talk*. London: Sage.

Harris, J. and Watson, E. D. (eds) (2007) *The Oprah Phenomenon*. Lexington: Kentucky University Press.

Hartley, J. (1992) *The Politics of Pictures.* London: Routledge.
Hartley, J. (1996) *Popular Journalism.* London: Arnold.
Hazlitt, W. (1991) On public opinion, in J. Cook (ed.), *William Hazlitt: Selected writings.* Oxford: Oxford University Press.
Hermes, J. (1997) Gender and media studies: no woman, no cry, in J. Corner, P. Schlesinger and R. Silverstone (eds), *International Media Research: A Critical Survey.* London: Routledge.
Higgins, M. (2006) Characterising a political public sphere in the Scottish press: a comparative analysis, *Journalism: Theory, Practice and Criticism,* 7: 25–44.
Higgins, M. (2008) The 'public inquisitor' as media celebrity, *Cultural Politics,* 4.
Hindess, B. and Hirst, P. (1977) *Mode of Production and Social Formation.* London: Macmillan.
Hobsbawm, E. (2007) *Globalisation, Democracy and Terrorism.* London: Little, Brown.
Hodge, R. and Kress, G. (1988) *Social Semiotics.* Cambridge: Polity.
Hodge, R. and Kress, G. (1993) *Language as Ideology,* 2nd edn. London: Routledge.
Hollander, B. A. (1997) Fuel to the fire: talk radio and the Gamson Hypothesis, *Political Communication,* 14: 355–69.
Homer (1980) *The Odyssey.* Oxford: Oxford University Press.
Horkheimer, M. ([1941] 1982) The end of reason, in A. Arato and E. Gebhardt (eds), *The Essential Frankfurt School Reader.* New York: Continuum.
Horton, D. and Wohl, R. (1982) Mass communication and para-social interaction: observations on intimacy, in G. Gumpert and R. Cathcart (eds), *Inter/media,* 2nd edn. New York: Oxford University Press.
Howard, P. H. (2006) *New Media Campaigns and the Managed Citizen.* Cambridge: Cambridge University Press.
Hutchby, I. (1991) The organization of talk on talk radio, in P. Scannell (ed.), *Broadcast Talk.* London: Sage.
Hutchby, I. (1996) Power in discourse: the case of arguments on a British talk radio show, *Discourse & Society,* 7: 481–97.
Hutchby, I. (2001) Confrontation as spectacle: the argumentative frame of the *Ricki Lake Show,* in A. Tolson (ed.), *Television Talk Shows: Discourse, Performance, Spectacle.* Mahwah, NJ: LEA.
Hutchby, I. (2006) *Media Talk: Conversation Analysis and the Study of Broadcasting.* Maidenhead: Open University Press.
Hutchinson, D. (1999) *Media Policy.* Oxford: Blackwell.
Iedema, R. (2001) Analysing film and television: a social semiotic account of *Hospital: An Unhealthy Business,* in T. van Leeuwen and C. Jewitt (eds), *Handbook of Visual Analysis.* London: Sage.

ITV (2003) *Trisha*, 30 Dec. ITV 1: London.

ITV (2006) *Jeremy Kyle Show*, 5 Dec. ITV 1: London.

Jameson, F. (1991) *Postmodernism, or, the Cultural Logic of Late Capitalism.* London: Verso.

Jefferson, T. (1946) *Thomas Jefferson on Democracy.* New York: New American Library.

Jensen, R. (2004) September 11 and the failures of American intellectuals, *Communication and Critical/Cultural Studies*, 1: 80–8.

Jensen, E. (2005) An anchor who reports disasters with a heart on his sleeve, *New York Times*, 12 Sep.

Johansson, S. (2007) 'They just make sense': tabloid newspapers as an alternative public sphere, in R. Butsch (ed.), *Media and Public Spheres.* Basingstoke: Palgrave Macmillan.

Jones, D. A. (1998) Political talk radio: the Limbaugh effect on primary voters, *Political Communication*, 15: 367–81.

Jones, J. P. (2005) *Entertaining Politics.* Oxford: Rowan and Littlefield.

Katz, E. (2006) Rediscovering Gabriel Tarde, *Political Communication*, 23: 263–70.

Katz, E. and Lazarsfeld, P. F. (1964) *Personal Influence.* New York: Free Press.

Kazin, M. (1995) *The Populist Persuasion: An American History.* New York: Basic Books.

Keane, J. (1991) *The Media and Democracy.* Cambridge: Polity Press.

Keane, J. (1995) Structural transformations of the public sphere, *The Communication Review*, 1: 1–22.

King, E. and Schudson, M. (1995) The press and the illusion of public opinion: the strange case of Ronald Reagan's 'popularity', in T. L. Glasser and C. T. Salmon (eds), *Public Opinion and the Communication of Consent.* New York: Guilford.

Kornhauser, W. (1960) *The Politics of Mass Society.* London: Routledge and Kegan Paul.

Kress, G. (1986) Language in the media: the construction of the domains of public and private, *Media, Culture & Society*, 8: 395–419.

Kress, G. and van Leeuwen, T. (2001) *Multimodal Discourse.* London: Arnold.

Kumar, K. (1977) Holding the middle ground: the BBC, the public and the professional broadcaster, in J. Curran, M. Gurevitch and J. Woollacott (eds), *Mass Communication and Society.* London: Edward Arnold.

Lance Holbert, R. (2004) Political talk radio, perceived fairness, and the establishment of George W. Bush's political legitimacy, *The Harvard International Journal of Press/Politics*, 9(3): 12–27.

Lasch, C. (1979) *The Culture of Narcissism.* New York: Norton.

Lavrakas, P. J. and Traugott, M. W. (2000) Election polling in the twenty-first century: challenges and opportunities, in P. J. Lavrakas and M. W. Traugott (eds), *Election Polls, the News Media, and Democracy*. New York: Seven Bridges.

Leach, E. (1976) *Culture and Communication*. Cambridge: Cambridge University Press.

Leavis, F. R. (1948) Mass civilisation and minority culture, *Education and the University*. London: Chatto and Windus.

Lee, G. and Cappella, J. N. (2001) The effects of political talk radio on political attitude formation: exposure versus knowledge, *Political Communication*, 18: 369–94.

Lees-Marshment, J. (2004) *The Political Marketing Revolution*. Manchester: Manchester University Press.

Levi-Strauss, C. ([1964] 1992) *The Raw and the Cooked: Introduction to a Science of Mythology*. Harmondsworth: Penguin.

Lewis, J. (2001) *Constructing Public Opinion*. New York: Columbia University Press.

Lewis, J., Inthorn, S. and Wahl-Jorgensen, K. (2005) *Citizens or Consumers? What the Media Tell us About Political Participation*. Maidenhead: Open University Press.

Lewis, J. and Wahl-Jorgensen, K. (2005) Active citizen or couch potato? Journalism and public opinion, in S. Allan (ed.), *Journalism: Critical Issues*. Maidenhead: Open University Press.

Lippmann, W. ([1927] 1993) *The Phantom Public*. New York: Transaction.

Lippmann, W. ([1922] 1997) *Public Opinion*. New York: Free Press.

Livingstone, S. (2005a) In defence of privacy: mediating the public/private boundary at home, in S. Livingstone (ed.), *Audiences and Publics*. Bristol: Intellect.

Livingstone, S. (2005b) On the relation between audiences and publics, in S. Livingstone (ed.), *Audiences and Publics*. Bristol: Intellect.

Livingstone, S. and Lunt, P. (1994) *Talk on Television*. London: Routledge.

Louw, E. (2005) *Media and Political Process*. London: Sage.

Lowenthal, L. (1961) *Literature, Popular Culture and Society*. Englewood Cliffs, NJ: Prentice Hall.

Lucas, J. R. (1976) *Democracy and Participation*. Harmondsworth: Penguin.

Lunt, P. and Stenner, P. (2005) The *Jerry Springer Show* as an emotional public sphere, *Media, Culture & Society*, 27: 59–81.

Lupton, D. (1998) *The Emotional Self: A Sociocultural Exploration*. London: Sage.

MacCabe, C. (1985) *Theoretical Essays*. Manchester: Manchester University Press.

Macdonell, D. (1986) *Theories of Discourse: An Introduction*. Oxford: Blackwell.

Macey, D. (2000) *The Penguin Dictionary of Critical Theory.* Harmondsworth: Penguin.

Madianou, M. (2005) The elusive public of television news, in S. Livingstone (ed.), *Audiences and Publics.* Bristol: Intellect.

Marshall, P. D. (1997) *Celebrity and Power.* Minneapolis: Minnesota University Press.

Martin, B. and Mohanty, C. (1988) Feminist politics: what's home got to do with it? in T. de Lauretis (ed.), *Feminist Studies/Critical Studies.* Basingstoke: Macmillan.

Matheson, D. (2005) *Media Discourses: Analysing Media Texts.* Maidenhead: Open University Press.

Matthews, N. (2007) Confessions to a new public, *Video Nation Shorts. Media, Culture and Society,* 29(3): 435–48.

Mayhew, L. H. (1997) *The New Public.* Cambridge: Cambridge University Press.

McCauley, M. P. (2002) The contested meaning of Public Service in American television, *The Communication Review,* 5: 207–37.

McChesney, R. W. (1999) *Rich Media, Poor Democracy.* New York: New Press.

McCombs, M. (1994) News influence on our pictures of the world, in J. Bryant and D. Zillmann (eds), *Media Effects: Advances in Theory and Research.* Hillsdale, NJ: LEA.

McGuigan, J. (1992) *Cultural Populism.* London: Routledge.

McGuigan, J. (1996) *Culture and the Public Sphere.* London: Routledge.

McGuigan, J. (2004) *Rethinking Cultural Policy.* Maidenhead: Open University Press.

McGuigan, J. (2005) The cultural public sphere, *European Journal of Cultural Studies,* 8: 427–43.

McLeod, D. M. and Hertog, J. K. (1992) The manufacture of 'public opinion' by reporters: informal cues for public perceptions of protest groups, *Discourse & Society,* 3: 259–75.

McNair, B. (2000) *Journalism and Democracy.* London: Routledge.

McNair, B. (2006) *Cultural Chaos.* London: Routledge.

McNair, B., Hibberd, M. and Schlesinger, P. (2002) Public access broadcasting and democratic participation in the age of mediated politics, *Journalism Studies,* 3: 407–22.

McNair, B., Hibberd, M. and Schlesinger, P. (2003) *Mediated Access.* Luton: Luton University Press.

McQuail, D. (1994) Mass communication and the public interest: towards a social theory for media structure and performance, in D. Crowley and D. Mitchell (eds), *Communication Theory Today.* Cambridge: Polity Press.

McQuail, D. (2003) *Media Accountability and Freedom of Publication.* Oxford: Oxford University Press.

McRobbie, A. (2004) Notes on *What Not to Wear* and post-feminist symbolic violence, *The Sociological Review*, 52: 99–109.

Media Matters (2004) Rush Limbaugh transcripts. Available at: http://mediamatters.org

Media Monitors (2004) Interview: John Howard, 15 Aug. Available at: http://sunday.ninemsn.com.au/sunday/political_transcripts/article_1622.asp

Meehan, E. R. (1990) Why we don't count: the commodity audience, in P. Mellencamp (ed.), *Logics of Television: Essays in Cultural Criticism*. Bloomington: Indiana University Press/BFI.

Meet the Press (1996) Transcripts. Available at: www.msnbc.msn.com/id/3032608/

Mehl, D. (2005) The public on the television screen: towards a public sphere of exhibition, in S. Livingstone (ed.), *Audiences and Publics*. Bristol: Intellect.

Mestrovic, S. G. (1997) *Postemotional Society*. Thousand Oaks, CA: Sage.

Metyková, M. (2003) Regulation of public service broadcasting: the European framework, in V. Štětka and J. Volek (eds), *Média a Realita*. Brno: Masaryk University Press.

Miles, S. (1998) *Consumerism As a Way of Life*. London: Sage.

Miliband, R. (1973) *The State in Capitalist Society*. London: Quartet.

Miller, P. V. (1995) The industry of public opinion, in T. L. Glasser and C. T. Salmon (eds) *Public Opinion and the Communication of Consent*. New York: Guilford.

Miller, D. (2002) Public relations and journalism: promotion and power, in A. Briggs and P. Cobley (eds), *The Media: An Introduction*. London: Longman.

Miller, D. (ed.) (2003) *Tell Me Lies: Propaganda and Media Distortion in the Attack on Iraq*. London: Pluto.

Mills, S. (1997) *Discourse*. London: Routledge.

Montgomery, M. (1986) DJ talk, *Media, Culture & Society*, 8: 421–40.

Montgomery, M. (1999) Talk as entertainment: the case of the *Mrs Merton Show*, in L. Haarman (ed.), *Talk About Shows: La Parola e lo Spettacolo*. Bolognia: CLUEB.

Montgomery, M. (2007) *The Discourse of Broadcast News*. London: Routledge.

Moon, N. (1999) *Opinion Polls: History, Theory and Practice*. Manchester: Manchester University Press.

Morley, D. (2000) *Home Territories: Media, Mobility and Identity*. London: Routledge.

Mosco, V. (1996) *The Political Economy of Communication*. London: Sage.

Moseley, R. (2000) Makeover takeover on British television, *Screen*, 41: 299–314.

Mullin, C. (2006) The media and political responsibility. Paper presented to the PSA, Media and Politics Group Annual Conference, University of Sunderland, 17–18 Nov.

Munnichs, G. (2004) Whom to trust? Public concerns, late modern risks, and expert trustworthiness, *Journal of Agricultural and Environmental Ethics*, 17: 113–30.

Murdock, G. (1992) Citizens, consumers and public culture, in M. Skovman and K. C. Schrøder (eds), *Media Cultures: Reappraising Transnational Media*. London: Routledge.

Murdock, G. (1994) Tales of expertise and experience: sociological reasoning and popular representation, in C. Haslam and A. Bryman (eds), *Social Scientists Meet the Media*. London: Routledge.

Myers, G. (2001) I'm out of it; you guys argue: making an issue of it on the *Jerry Springer Show*, in A. Tolson (ed.), *Television Talk Shows: Discourse, Performance, Spectacle*. Mahwah, NJ: LEA.

Naylor, R., Driver, S. and Cornford, J. (2000) The BBC goes online: public service broadcasting in the new media age, in D. Gauntlett (ed.), *Web.Studies*. London: Arnold.

Neale, S. (2001) Genre and television, in G. Creeber (ed.), *The Television Genre Book*. London: BFI.

Neveu, E. (2005) Politicians without politics, a polity without citizens: the politics of the chat show in contemporary France, *Modern and Contemporary France*, 13: 323–35.

Nolan, D. (2006) Media, citizenship and governmentality: defining 'the public' of public service broadcasting, *Social Semiotics*, 16: 225–42.

Norris, P. (2000) *A Virtuous Cycle*. Cambridge: Cambridge University Press.

O'Keeffe, A. (2006) *Interpreting Media Discourse*. Abingdon: Routledge.

Örnebring, H. (2007) A necessary profession for the modern age? Nineteenth century news, journalism and the public sphere, in R. Butsch (ed.), *Media and Public Spheres*. London: Palgrave.

Osborne, T. (2003) Against 'creativity': a philistine rant, *Economy and Society*, 32: 507–25.

Page, B. I. and Tannenbaum, J. (1996) Populistic deliberation and talk radio, *Journal of Communication*, 46(2): 33–54.

Palmer, G. (2003) *Discipline and Liberty: Television and Governance*. Manchester: Manchester University Press.

Pan, Z. and Kosicki, G. M. (1997) Talk show exposure as an opinion activity, *Political Communication*, 14: 371–88.

Paterson, C. (1998) Global battlefields, in O. Boyd-Barrett and T. Rantanen (eds), *The Globalization of News*. London: Sage.

Patrona, M. (2006) Conversationalization and media empowerment in Greek television discussion programs, *Discourse & Society*, 17: 5–27.

Patterson, T. E. (2005) Of polls, mountains: US journalists and their use of election surveys, *Public Opinion Quarterly*, 69: 716–24.

Pêcheux, M. (1988) Discourse: structure or event, in C. Nelson and L. Grossberg (eds), *Marxism and the Interpretation of Culture*. Urbana: Indiana University Press.

Peters, J. D. (1995) Historical tensions in the concept of public opinion, in T. L. Glasser and C. T. Salmon (eds), *Public Opinion and the Communication of Consent*. New York: Guilford.

Peters, J. D. (1999) *Speaking into the Air: A History of the Idea of Communication*. Chicago: Chicago University Press.

Philo, G. and Miller, D. (2001) Cultural compliance, in G. Philo and D. Miller (eds), *Market Killing*. Harlow: Longman.

Pigott, C. (1795) *A Political Dictionary: Explaining the True Meaning of Words*. London: D. I. Eaton.

Pilger, J. (2006) The moral mirror, *Free Press*, 150: 1.

Popper, K. ([1954] 1992) Public opinion and liberal principles, *In Search of a Better World: Lectures and Essays From Thirty Years*. London: Routledge.

Poster, M. (1997) Cyberdemocracy: the Internet and the public sphere, in D. Holmes (ed.), *Virtual Politics: Identity and Community in Cyberspace*. London: Sage.

Postman, N. (1987) *Amusing ourselves to death*. London: Methuen.

Priest, P. J. (1995) *Public Intimacies: Talk Show Participants and Tell-All TV*. Cresskill, NJ: Hampton.

Pusey, M. (1987) *Jürgen Habermas*. London: Ellis Norwood/Tavistock.

Rainey, L. (1998) *Institutions of Modernism*. New Haven: Yale University Press.

Ransom, J. S. (1997) *Foucault's Discipline: The Politics of Subjectivity*. Durham, NC: Duke University Press.

Rawls, J. (1996) *Political Liberalism*. New York: Columbia University Press.

Raymond, G. (2000) The voice of authority: the local accomplishment of authoritative discourse in live news broadcasts, *Discourse Studies*, 2: 354–79.

Reese, S. D., Rutigliano, L., Hyun, K. and Jeong, J. (2007) Mapping the blogosphere: professional and citizen-based news media in the global news, *Journalism*, 8(3): 235–61.

Rhodes, R. A. W. (1997) *Understanding Governance*. Buckingham: Open University Press.

Rogers, L. (1949) *The Pollsters*. New York: Knopf.

Rose, N. (1999) *Powers of Freedom*. Cambridge: Cambridge University Press.

Rose, M. (2000) Through the eyes of *Video Nation*, in J. Izod, R. Kilborn and M. Hibberd (eds), *From Grierson to the Docu-Soap: Breaking the Boundaries*. Luton: Luton University Press.

Rosen, J. (1991) Making journalism more public, *Communication*, 12: 267–84.

Rowe, D. (2004) *Sport, Culture and the Media*, 2nd edn. Maidenhead: Open University Press.

Rubin, A. M. (1994) Media uses and effects: a uses-and-gratifications perspective, in J. Bryant and D. Zillmann (eds), *Media Effects: Advances in Theory and Research*. Hillsdale, NJ: LEA.

Rubin, A. M., Haridakis, P. M. and Eyal, K. (2003) Viewer aggression and attraction to television talk shows, *Media Psychology*, 5: 331–62.

Sacks, H. (1984) On doing 'being ordinary', in J. M. Atkinson and J. Heritage (eds), *Structures of Social Action: Studies in Conversation Analysis*. Cambridge: Cambridge University Press.

Said, E. W. (1994) *Representations of the Intellectual*. London: Vintage.

Samson, A. (1992) *F. R. Leavis*. Hemel Hempstead: Harvester Wheatsheaf.

Sandvoss, C. (2007) Public sphere and publicness: sport audiences and political discourse, in R. Butsch (ed.), *Media and Public Spheres*. Basingstoke: Palgrave Macmillan.

Sapiro, V. (2002) It's the context, situation and question, stupid: the gender basis of public opinion, in B. Norrander and C. Wilcox (eds), *Understanding Public Opinion*, 2nd edn. Washington: Congressional Quarterly Press.

Savigny, H. (2004) Media and the personal lives of politicians in the United States, *Parliamentary Affairs*, 57: 223–35.

Savigny, H. (2008) *The Problem of Political Marketing*. London: Continuum.

Scammell, M. (2003) Citizen consumers: towards a new marketing of politics? in J. Corner and D. Pels (eds), *Media and the Restyling of Politics*. London: Sage.

Scannell, P. (1990) Public service broadcasting: the history of a concept, in A. Goodwin and G. Whannel (eds), *Understanding Television*. London: Routledge.

Scannell, P. (1991) Introduction: the relevance of talk, in P. Scannell (ed.), *Broadcast Talk*. London: Sage.

Scannell, P. (1992) Public service broadcasting and modern public life, in P. Scannell, P. Schlesinger and C. Sparks (eds), *Culture and Power: A Media, Culture & Society Reader*. London: Sage.

Scannell, P. (1996) *Radio, Television and Modern Life*. Blackwell: Oxford.

Scheuer, J. (2001) *The Sound Bite Society*. New York: Routledge.

Schiffrin, D. (1987) *Discourse Markers*. Cambridge: Cambridge University Press.

Schudson, M. (1995) *The Power of News*. Cambridge, MA: Harvard University Press.

Scott, G. G. (1996) *Can We Talk? The Power and Influence of Talk Shows*. New York: Insight.

Scruton, R. (2005) *Modern Culture*. London: Continuum.

Sennett, R. (2002) *The Fall of Public Man*. Cambridge: Cambridge University Press.

Seymore-Ure, C. (1968) *The Press, Politics and the Public*. London: Methuen.

Shattuc, J. (1997) *The Talking Cure: TV Talk Shows and Women*. London: Routledge.

Shattuc, J. (2001) The confessional talk show, in G. Creeber (ed.), *The Television Genre Book*. London: BFI.

Siltanen, J. and Stanworth, M. (eds) (1984) *Women and the Public Sphere*. London: Hutchison.

Simon-Vandenbergen, A. M. (2007) Lay and expert voices in public participation programmes: a case of generic heterogeneity, *Journal of Pragmatics*, 39: 1420–35.

Singer, J. (2005) The political j-blogger: 'normalizing' a new media form to fit old norms and practices, *Journalism*, 6(2): 173–98.

Slade, C. (2002) *The Real Thing: Doing Philosophy With Media*. New York: Peter Lang.

Slevin, J. (2000) *The Internet and Society*. Cambridge: Polity.

Smith, A. (2005) Lifestyle television programmes and the construction of the expert host, 3rd Language, Communication, Culture International Conference, University of Evora, Portugal, 23–5 Nov.

Snow, C. P. (1993) *The Two Cultures*. Cambridge: Cambridge University Press.

Staeheli, L. A. and Mitchell, D. (2004) Spaces of public and private: locating politics, in C. Barnett and M. Low (eds) *Spaces of Democracy*. London: Sage.

Stanley, A. (2006) In the evening news derby, CBS is betting on folksy, *New York Times*, 26 Feb.

Starkey, G. (2004) Radio Five Live: extending choice through Radio Bloke, in A. Crisell (ed.), *More than a Music Box*. London: Berghahn.

Starkey, G. (2007) *Balance and Bias in Journalism*. Basingstoke: Palgrave Macmillan.

Stedman Jones, G. (1982) Working-class culture and working-class politics in London, 1870–1900: notes on the remaking of a working class, in B. Waites, T. Bennett and G. Martin (eds), *Popular Culture: Past and Present*. London: Croon Helm.

Storey, J. (1985) Matthew Arnold: the politics of an organic intellectual, *Literature and History*, 11: 217–28.

Storey, J. (2003) *Inventing Popular Culture*. Oxford: Blackwell.

Street, J. (2001) *Mass Media, Politics and Democracy*. London: Palgrave.

Street, J. (2003) The celebrity politician: political style and popular culture, in J. Corner and D. Pels (eds), *Media and the Restyling of Politics*. London: Sage.

Street, J. (2004) Celebrity politicians: popular culture and political representation, *British Journal of Politics and International Relations*, 6: 435–52.

Street, J (2005a) Politics lost, politics transformed, politics colonized? Theories of the impact of mass media, *Political Studies Review*, 3(1): 17–33.

Street, J. (2005b) Showbusiness of a serious kind: the cultural politics of the arts prize, *Media, Culture and Society*, 27(6): 819–40.

Striphas, T. (2003) A dialectic with the everyday: communication and cultural politics on Ophrah Winfrey's Book Club, *Critical Studies in Media Communication*, 20: 295–316.

Stubbs, W. (1874) *The Constitutional History of England: In its Origin and Development, Volume One*. Oxford: Clarendon.

Stubbs, M. (1983) *Discourse Analysis*. Oxford: Blackwell.

Talbot, M. (2007) *Media Discourse: Representation and Interaction*. Edinburgh: Edinburgh University Press.

Taylor, C. (1995) *Philosophical Arguments*. Cambridge, MA: Harvard University Press.

Taylor, L. (2002) From ways of life to lifestyle: the 'ordinari-ization' of British gardening lifestyle television, *European Journal of Cultural Studies*, 17: 479–93.

Temple, M. (2000) New Labour's third way: pragmatism and governance, *British Journal of Politics and International Relations*, 2: 302–25.

Temple, M. (2006) Dumbing down is good for you, *British Politics*, 1(2): 257–73.

Thompson, J. B. (1995) *The Media and Modernity*. Cambridge: Polity.

Thornborrow, J. (2001a) Authenticating talk: building public identities in audience participation programming, *Discourse Studies*, 3: 459–79.

Thornborrow, J. (2001b) Has it ever happened to you? Talk show stories as mediated performance, in A. Tolson (ed.), *Television Talk Shows: Discourse, Performance Spectacle*. Mahwah, NJ: LEA.

Thornborrow, J. (2002) *Power Talk*. Harlow: Pearson.

Tolson, A. (1991) Televised chat and the synthetic personality, in P. Scannell (ed.), *Broadcast Talk*. London: Sage.

Tolson, A. (ed.) (2001) *Television Talk Shows: Discourse, Performance, Spectacle*. Mahwah, NJ: LEA.

Tolson, A. (2006) *Media Talk: Spoken Discourse on TV and Radio*. Edinburgh: Edinburgh University Press.

Trepte, S. (2005) Daily talk as self-realization: an empirical study on participation in daily talk shows, *Media Psychology*, 7: 165–89.

Tuchman, G. (1972) Objectivity as strategic ritual: an examination of newsmen's notions of objectivity, *American Journal of Sociology*, 77: 660–79.

Van Dijk, T. A. (1998) *Ideology: A Multidisciplinary Approach*. London: Sage.

Van Ginneken, J. (1998) *Understanding Global News*. London: Sage.

Van Leeuwen, T. (2001) Semiotics and iconography, in T. van Leeuwen and C. Jewitt (eds), *Handbook of Visual Analysis*. London: Sage.

Van Leeuwen, T. and Jewitt, C. (2001) *Handbook of Visual Analysis*. London: Sage.

Wahl-Jorgensen, K. (1999) Letters to the editor, *Peace Review*, 11: 53–9.

Wahl-Jorgensen, K. (2002a) The construction of the public in letters to the editor: deliberative democracy and the idiom of insanity, *Journalism*, 3: 183–204.

Wahl-Jorgensen, K. (2002b) The normative-economic justification for public discourse: letters to the editor as a 'wide open' forum, *Journalism and Mass Communication Quarterly*, 79: 121–33.

Wahl-Jorgensen, K. (2002c) Understanding the conditions for public discourse: four rules for selecting letters to the editor, *Journalism Studies*, 3: 69–81.

Waltz, M. (2005) *Alternative and Activist Media*. Edinburgh: Edinburgh University Press.

Warner, M. (2002) *Publics and Counterpublics*. New York: Zone.

Weber, M. ([1919] 1971) Politics as a vocation, in A. Pizzorno (ed.), *Political Sociology*. Harmondsworth: Penguin.

Weber, B. R. (2005) Beauty, desire and anxiety: the economy of sameness on ABC's *Extreme Makeover*, *Genders Online Journal*, 41.

Wessler, H. and Schultz, T. (2007) Can the mass media deliberate? Insights from print media and political talk shows, in R. Butsch (ed.), *Media and Public Spheres*. Basingstoke: Palgrave Macmillan.

Whillock, R. K. (1999) Giant sucking sounds: politics as illusion, in D. Slayden and R. K. Whillock (eds), *Soundbite Culture*. Thousand Oaks: Sage.

Wilhoit, G. C. and Weaver, W. ([1980] 1990) *Newsroom Guide to Polls and Surveys*. Bloomington: Indiana University Press.

Williams, K. (1998) *Get Me a Murder a Day*. London: Arnold.

Williams, R. (1961) *The Long Revolution*. London: Chatto and Windus.

Williams, R. (1981) *Culture*. London: Fontana.

Williams, R. (1983) *Keywords: A Vocabulary of Culture and Society*. London: Fontana.

Wilson, J. (1990) *Politically Speaking*. Oxford: Basil Blackwell.

Wood, H. (2001) No, YOU rioted! The pursuit of conflict in the management of 'Lay' and 'Expert' discourses on *Kilroy*, in A. Tolson (ed.), *Television Talk Shows: Discourse, Performance, Spectacle*. Mahwah, NJ: LEA.

Yanovitzky, I. and Cappella, J. N. (2001) Effect of call-in political talk radio shows on their audiences: evidence from a multi-wave panel analysis, *International Journal of Public Opinion Research*, 13: 377–97.

Young, I. M. (1990) *Justice and the Politics of Difference*. Princeton: Princeton University Press.

Young, I. M. (1997) *Intersecting Voices*. Princeton: Princeton University Press.

Index

KEY THEMES IN MEDIA THEORY

Dan Laughey

"Key Themes in Media Theory is wonderfully wide-ranging and deservedly destined to become a key text for students of Media Studies."
Professor John Storey, University of Sunderland, UK

"The very best text books are not just summaries of complex ideas for a student audience or an introduction to a critical canon; the very best add something to the canon they reflect upon, and Dan Laughey's Key Themes in Media Theory is one such book. [It] is not a means to an end, as many such books can be. Rather it is a motivational primer, and one that should send both students and teachers heading to the library to read the theorists presented here again, for the first time."
Richard Berger, Art, Design, Media; The Higher Education Academy, UK

- What is media theory?
- How do media affect our actions, opinions and beliefs?
- In what ways do media serve powerful political and economic interests?
- Is media consumerism unhealthy or is it empowering?

Key Themes in Media Theory provides a thorough and critical introduction to the key theories of media studies. It is unique in bringing together different schools of media theory into a single, comprehensive text, examining in depth the ideas of key media theorists such as Lasswell, McLuhan, Hall, Williams, Barthes, Adorno, Baudrillard and Bourdieu.

Using up-to-date case studies the book embraces media in their everyday cultural forms – music, internet, film, television, radio, newspapers and magazines – to enable a clearer view of the 'big picture' of media theory.

In ten succinct chapters Dan Laughey discusses a broad range of themes, issues and perspectives that inform our contemporary understanding of media production and consumption. These include:

- Behaviourism and media effects
- Feminist media theory
- Postmodernity and information society
- Political economy
- Media consumerism

With images and diagrams to illustrate chapter themes, examples that apply media theory to media practice, recommended reading at the end of every chapter, and a useful glossary of key terms, this book is the definitive guide to understanding media theory.

Contents: *List of figures and illustrations – Acknowledgements – What is media theory? – Behaviourism and media effects – Modernity and medium theory – Structuralism and semiotics – Interactionism and structuration – Feminisms and gender – Political economy and postcolonial theory – Postmodernity and information society – Consumerism and everyday life – Debating media theory – Glossary – References.*

2007 248pp
978-0-335-21813-4 (Paperback)   978-0-335-21814-1 (Hardback)

THE BRITISH PRESS

Mick Temple

"Mick Temple's book makes an important contribution to the debate on the critical historical role and uncertain future of newspapers and the key place of quality journalism within that debate."
Jeremy Dear, General Secretary of the National Union of Journalists, UK

"This book provides a brilliant synthesis of academic and journalistic debate on the past, present and future of the British newspaper. Impressively up-to-date, it is an accessible and well sign-posted introduction to students of the news media and political communication and should become an essential addition to their reading."
Martin Conboy, University of Sheffield, UK

"A thorough and thoughtful investigation into the British press and its contribution to our social and political culture."
Simon Kelner, Editor-in-Chief, The Independent

This exciting book offers a practical introduction to the history, theory, politics and potential future of British newspapers. Focussing on the relationship between the press and political history, it examines their social and political impact, assessing the press's contribution to enlarging and informing the public sphere.

The author provides a theoretical critique of press developments. The first part of the text leads you through key historical moments from the English Civil War to Wapping and beyond, while the second half takes an in-depth look at current empirical and theoretical concerns. Scholarly yet accessible, Mick Temple is not afraid to take a position on today's contentious issues.

The book takes a more positive perspective on the British press than has often been the case, highlighting the online strength of great brand names like the Telegraph, Guardian, Sun and Mail. Temple argues that throughout their history, our newspapers have been vital conduits for public opinion and, on occasion, catalysts for social change.

The British Press is key reading for journalism, media and social science students.

Contents: *Acknowledgements – Introduction – From Gutenberg to mass medium – The shock of the new: the rise of the 'popular press' – The press and the Second World War: the triumph of radio – The post-war press and the decline of deference . . . and sales – New technology: Wapping and beyond – The local press – Theories of news production and news values – Censorship – Spin, public relations and the press – Newspapers and 'dumbing down' – The press and democracy: speaking for the public? – Future imperfect? – Bibliography – Index.*

2008 272pp
978-0-335-22297-1 (Paperback)   978-0-335-22298-8 (Hardback)

UNDERSTANDING THE LOCAL MEDIA

Meryl Aldridge

- How will local media deal with the challenge of the Internet?
- How important is regional news to the nations of the UK?
- What does the future hold for newspapers, regional television and local radio news?

Most adults in the UK read a local newspaper; regional news bulletins are among the most-watched on television; and local radio has a loyal following. This is hardly surprising as, for most people, the everyday activities of life take place within familiar local territory.

Even though the majority of political and economic decisions affecting daily life are taken far away and are shaped by global processes, their impact is experienced locally. Local media are vital if there is to be an effective arena for informed debate about these issues. But despite being both popular and politically important, local media are often overlooked on media-related courses and in discussions of the role of the media in contemporary society.

Understanding the Local Media addresses this gap by explaining how regional newspapers and broadcast news are owned, regulated and organized; how these factors produce the outputs we see and hear; what we know of audiences' attitude to them; and discusses local media as places of work.

Meryl Aldridge brings issues alive by the extensive use of real examples and offers a fascinating insight into this media sector for students and teachers on academic and professional media courses. It also provides stimulating reading for anyone interested in UK media today.

Contents: *Introduction – Why local media matter – Regional and local newspapers: Just another retailer? – Imagining the community – Local broadcasting: What price public service? – Must regional news be anodyne? – A delicate balance: Media in the nations of the UK – Working in local media: From smoke-filled rooms to sweatshops – What is the future for local media? – References – Index.*

2007 208pp
978-0-335-22172-1 (Paperback)   978-0-335-22173-8 (Hardback)